SECURITY IN THE YEAR 2000 AND BEYOND

by
Louis A. Tyska, Lawrence J. Fennelly
and Associates

An ETC Publication

Illustrations

Dover Publications, Inc.
Mineola, N.Y.
Selected by Jim Harter

Library of Congress Cataloging in Publication Data
Security in the year 2000 and beyond.
  1. Private security services — United States.
2. Private security services — United States — Management. 3. Twenty-first century — Forecasts. I. Tyska, Louis A., 1934-   . II. Fennelly, Lawrence J., 1940-
HV8290.S374 1987   363.2'89'0973   86-16694
ISBN 0-88280-117-1

Published by ETC Publications
              Palm Springs
              California 92263-1608

DEDICATION

To all of those people who have worked so hard in the past to bring our profession to the springboard of the future.

CONTENTS

INTRODUCTION

Why a collection of essays written by security professionals about the future? This question was asked frequently of the editors when developing and editing this work.

Because we collectively are preparing an emerging discipline to take its rightful place in the business management structure, is only one of several reasons. Security managers stand on a foundation of only recently being "accepted" by business management and certainly not by all. If we are to be truly accepted into the cadre of business leadership, we need to prepare in several ways; the most critical of which is what is ahead.

The knowledge of where we have come from as a profession and where we are, is overshadowed by the need to know and plan for where we are heading in the future. This look into the future by these leading professionals may not be the direction of the asset protection field totally, but surely is a stimulus to each individual professional to consider the future.

In putting this book together, it was our intent to stimulate thought, direction and discussion for the future. Those that participated were asked to analyze the present, set five year goals for the next fifteen years and examine the future.

For many of us the years 2000 and beyond will be exciting years. The growth of technology as we see it today will have matured. In 1939 Buck Rogers and Flash Gordon were only movie screen characters. Today we see the space shuttle making trips into outer space approximately every two months.

We feel it is the responsibility of the security professional of today stimulate thought for those who follow in the future. It is our wish that this work will serve as a planning aid for the professionals and managers concerned with crime prevention and asset protection. It is also a goal that students of Business, Economics, Law, Humanities and Criminal Justice will gain a futuristic perspective from the thoughts expressed by contributors.

Insight to the future is knowledge; to be proud with knowledge is to be blind with light.

Louis A. Tyska
Lawrence J. Fennelly

1

Industry Trends
Security World

Few industries remain static over time, and the security industry is no exception.

In fact, security may prove to be more dynamic than any other sector of the economy. While corporations and industries adjust to the changing nature of business and the causes behind crime, security must anticipate these changes and be ready to meet them before they occur. The reason why is in the nature of security itself. It must prevent loss rather than react to it.

Some of the changes that security professionals and security management will face in the coming years will be specific to their own industry sector. But all of the sectors will share some common changes and challenges in the years ahead.

For example, all of the security professionals will be affected in their approach to physical security by trends and changes in security systems, fire protection systems and fire codes. As computers become more ingrained in the tactics of doing business, they will face a new type of computer crime, and a new type of white collar criminal.

As a tight economy makes a demand to take additional steps to reduce losses and conserve profits, companies will make attempts to stop the potential for loss at some of its sources. A greater use of employee screening and testing will help to keep potential wrongdoers from ever going to work for a company. A greater awareness of insurance, and new types of insurance policies, will help companies recover from the financial impact of a security problem if other measures are attempted and fail.

But even in the midst of an impartial business and electronic environment, security will still have a personal side. A greater availability of security education and training, both at the college level and in practical courses for the working security practitioner, will foster a new generation of security administrators and security officers. This, in turn, will foster changing patterns in the use of contract and proprietary security guards, and how those guards interface with electronic systems in a broader security program. And those programs will not overlook the individual while they are protecting assets, information and property. People will be protected from the various personal threats they will face in tomorrow's world.

On the following pages, *Security World* examines these areas of common security interest and takes a look at some of the trends happening in them. Probable future developments are also identified, and their impact assessed.

It's all designed to help you, the security professional and practitioner, get a better grasp today on what will be expected from you tomorrow.

Security Systems

The past few years have seen an increasing reliance on electronic security systems by business and industry, and the foreseeable future is not likely to see any change in that trend.

In fact, electronic security systems are likely to be an even more important part of security programs in the future. As

10

companies become more conscious of maintaining bottom line profits, electronic systems will be viewed with increasing value as a means to secure a facility or extend the surveillance capabilities of contract or proprietary security guard services. This trend can already be seen in the federal sector, where the Federal Protective Service will be placing increased reliance on electronic security systems in the future.

But how much is private sector spending for electronic security systems and equipment likely to increase? A *Security World* survey of corporate executives' attitudes on security (October, 1981) can provide some idea. About 57 percent of the respondents said they expected spending to increase between 5 percent and 25 percent over the next five years. Almost 24 percent said they expected spending to increase by more than 25 percent for the same period.

As a part of the same survey, the executives were also asked where they thought it was most important to invest company funds in the next 24 months. About 68 percent of the respondents said security equipment, about 35 percent said energy management systems, and about 26 percent said fire protection equipment.

An indication of what kinds of security equipment will be installed can be found in an earlier study (February, 1981). Security directors were asked what types of equipment where likely to experience increased use in the next five years. In descending order, their most often mentioned choices were CCTV systems, access controls, local alarm systems, locks, smoke detectors, fire suppression systems, space protection devices, fire detectors, perimeter protection devices and proprietary central stations.

Changing Technologies

Apart from increased equipment use in the next decade, the security industry will see some changes in the technology of the equipment being used. For Gene Fuss of Honeywell, the changes will take place in terms of detector sensing and alarm communications. For Garrett Lion, a consultant with the management systems consulting firm of Arthur D. Little,

Inc., of San Francisco, the changes will take place in terms of the integration of technologies and the integration of systems functions.

"You won't see many changes in terms of the method by which a sensor detects an alarm," Fuss said. "Most of the ways that is done have proved adequate. But you will see changes in the way the signal is processed out of the sensor. That will be a result of intelligence that is built into the individual sensors."

On the security side, Fuss said, much of the new technology will be directed toward keeping false alarm rates down. This will be done through a sensor's built-in ability to process its own signal. By some form of signature recognition or analog processing, the sensor will be able to assess the disturbance pattern it is recording, and determine whether the disturbance is due to the presence of a human intruder, meriting an alarm signal, or a non-human intruder or an act of nature, meriting no response.

"To do this, intelligence could be built into the sensor, or an analog signal could be sent back to a 'black box' at the central control point," Fuss said. "The limiting factors in this case would be economics in terms of what the sensors and the processors would cost."

Fuss said this type of signal processing could find particularly strong applications in the area of outdoor or perimeter alarm systems, where false alarms due to acts of nature occur frequently.

Alarm Communications

The next decade should also see an improvement in alarm communications, both in terms of the communications channel itself, and in speed and flexibility with which alarms are communicated to central monitoring points.

"Government standards are very poor on this point, and they should not be," Fuss said. "The intruder has an option. He doesn't have to bother beating the alarm sensors if he can beat the alarm communications lines. Fortunately, this is a problem encountered only in terms of high security applications or the targets of extremely sophisticated thieves."

The future will see the security industry seeking new avenues of alarm communications, Fuss said. Radio frequency alarm transmission is already available. Fiber-optic cables will also provide an opportunity for signal transmission. Even the live power lines already in place in a functioning building could be used to transmit alarm signals.

However, the key to the success and reliability of these communications channels will be their ability to be supervised on a constant basis, assuring system integrity against any failure or tap.

"In terms of communications flexibility, multiplexing is a step toward the future," Fuss said. "With it, a number of remote panels can be hooked to one pair of wires and report an alarm back to the central control. As multiplexing speed increases, you'll see more and more devices hooked to the paired wire. There will even be a multiplexing of the specific detectors themselves."

The final improvement in alarm communications will be in the central processors and computers controlling the system, Fuss said.

"If you have one computer handling everything, including energy management in an integrated system, you can have some major problems if the computer breaks down," he said. "You can avoid this by using dual processors, separating the control response for fire/security and energy management. And you will still have a master computer controlling both."

There may be a premium cost involved in this type of digital distributed computer control system, Fuss said, but the premium may be justified if the system can achieve the level of security and meet the reliability needs of the user.

The Push for Integration

Using dual processors for fire security and energy monitoring control is another means to integrate building systems functions. And the move toward systems integration will be one of the main trends in the security industry in the 1980s, according to Garrett Lion.

Security World research studies tend to support Lion's observations. In a survey of corporate executives (October, 1981), more than 54 percent of the respondents said their fire and security systems were currently integrated, and an additional 18 percent said they expected to integrate their systems at some time in the future. In a survey of security directors on their equipment retrofitting practices, about 11 percent of the respondents said their security and energy management systems were integrated. Of those currently lacking integrated systems, more than 30 percent said they expected the systems to be integrated within the next five years.

"As this type of integration increases, you'll see a push for more systems reliability through redundant installations and the use of more reliable uninterruptable power sources," Lion said.

As systems integration increases, the interface between the system operator and the equipment at the control panel will become more important. Accordingly, Lion said, operator controls are likely to become more "user friendly" in the future. This will essentially allow the user to operate the system in a simpler, quicker and more efficient manner.

Another major trend for the decade will be the integration of technologies, that is, using the same piece of physical equipment to do more than one job. This trend will be fueled by increasing user awareness of security and fire protection needs, and the increased retrofitting of fire and security systems to meet needs.

"Consider an existing building and the need to retrofit security and fire systems into it," Lion said. "That can be a costly proposition, so you may want to use some of the existing wiring in the building, or use a new wiring system for more than one purpose."

As an example, Lion cited a hotel that might be installing an advanced phone system. Apart from using the lines for voice communications, the system could also be used to transmit fire or panic alarms from guest rooms, alarm signals to the individual rooms, or voice evacuation instructions to hotel guests in the event of a fire.

The limiting factors in this type of installation would be in terms of code restrictions on the integrity of the wiring system, he said. The lines might have to be supervised, and would probably have to be protected against damage to ensure operation in the event of a fire emergency.

In any event, security technology will advance in the next decade, and the net effect of that advancement will be to provide improved security and fire protection, more reliable monitoring capabilities, and a quicker and more effective response to emergency situations.

Fire Control

Fire awareness is at an all time high. Within the last decade, the federal government has increased its attention to the fire problem by establishing the U.S. Fire Administration and by expanding the National Bureau of Standards' fire-related research programs. More recently, state and local governments have begun to scrutinize their fire safety codes, and many of them have made or are in the process of revising or expanding codes.

In the private sector, business and industry have had their eyes opened quickly to the potential losses and legal entanglements due to fire. Several major hotel fires within the past two years have awakened them to the realization that similar losses could happen to them.

Corporate Awareness

A February, 1981, *Security World* survey of security directors in the commercial, industrial and institutional sectors indicated that fire and smoke detectors and fire suppression are widely used, and that the equipment is replaced or upgraded approximately every 2 to 2 ½ years. More than one-half of the respondents said that their plans over the next five years call for increased use and/or upgrading of equipment.

In an October, 1981 *Security World* survey of corporate executives, of the respondents who said their companies use fire detection/suppression systems, 82.5 percent felt that their systems were adequate or more than adequate.

15

The two important issues in fire prevention are high-rise fire code revisions and mandatory sprinkler systems. This is where the activity in the fire prevention arena has been occurring and is likely to cause the most activity in the future.

"Cities and states are beginning to realize the need for practical fire protection," said George O'Rourke of Schirmer Engineering, fire protection consultants in Deerfield, Ill. As a result, there has been a trend to incorporate more fire protection into building codes. Houston, Las Vegas and the state of California are examples of places where local governments are getting tougher when it concerns fire protection. California has been studying a retrofit code, and Clark County, Nev., site of the MGM Grand Hotel fire, now requires retrofitting of hotel structures.

There also seems to be a general movement toward conformity to National Fire Protection Association codes. Many municipalities and private firms are beginning to look beyond achieving only minimum required protection. "The NFPA codes have always been there, and they have been adequate to prevent some of the major fires we've seen recently," a spokesperson for the NFPA said. But the codes are voluntary and, unless they are adopted by individual jurisdictions, building compliance with anything but minimum protection requirements is not necessary.

New Development

Although fire systems do not become obsolete if they still protect what they were originally intended to protect, modern technology continues to create new fire hazards that fire technology must contend with. And newer systems are always being developed to improve older systems, doing the same job for less money and in less space.

One of these newer systems is an improved high-challenge sprinkler system for industrial applications. This sprinkler is designed to suppress fires originating in densely concentrated combustible material, such as rolled paper, by giving off larger water droplets than conventional sprinklers. The larger droplets ensure that water will reach the fire, rather than being vaporized or blown upwards in drafts created by the fire. Other sprinkler developments will be those developed to comply with a specific NFPA standard for light fire hazards.

Another likely trend, O'Rourke said, is a change in the residential fire market. "There will be residential sprinkler systems in the future, perhaps within five years, most certainly before the end of the century."

The use of other fire suppression systems is also on the increase. As businesses invest more in high value computer and data processing equipment, they invest more in Halon and other dry chemical systems to protect them without the possibility of water damage.

Where There's Smoke

Most of the recent fire prevention activity concerns high-rise structures. One of the issues of high-rise fire safety that municipalities, engineers, and building owners and officials are wrestling with is the control of smoke. One of the stumbling blocks here is that "it is difficult to design smoke control into a building unless you know what is going to be burning," said Randall Tucker, director of the Houston office of Rolf Jensen and Associates, fire protection engineers.

Smoke control will receive more discussion in the future, Gerald O'Rourke said. Whatever is resolved will most likely go beyond equipment and involve building design, perhaps even the finish and furnishings.

"We can build a 'safe' building," Tucker said, "but we can't control what happens when the building is occupied. The fire hazard is really created by the habits of the individuals in that building, operating procedures and furnishings."

Concern About Toxicity

Many of a building's interior finishing materials and furnishings are made at least partly from plastics. When smoldering or burning, some of those plastics produce toxic gases. The issue of toxic gas in a fire is becoming as much or more of a concern than smoke, because these gases can kill before anyone realizes that a fire has started.

17

The problem from a fire prevention standpoint is how to deal with the sources of these gases. A building's finish can be regulated by building codes. Furnishings, however, come under the local fire code, and the regulation or control of building furnishings is a formidable task.

Attack on Arson

Arson task forces, a growing nationwide trend to combat this problem, have already achieved some victories. In the past year, the state of Arizona realized a 9 percent reduction in arson, and New Jersey was able to uncover several million dollars in fraudulent insurance claims thanks to an arson control program. These task forces are organized on both the state and local levels and are made up of police, prosecutors and private industry, including insurance companies working together to cut arson incidents and losses. Another new and growing trend in the field of arson prevention and detection are Arson Information Management Systems (AIMS), which help identify potential problems as well as help in the investigation of suspected arson incidents. The AIMS programs have been implements in several cities on a trial basis.

Finding a Balance

For the future, the NFPA sees a change in the traditional heavy reliance on public fire departments for immediate fire control. Not only is the cost of maintaining fire departments increasing, but inflation is also increasing the amount of losses in even small fires.

"A re-evaluation of the balance between public and private expenditures for fire protection" has been called for by the NFPA.

The cost of suppression after a fire has started can only be decreased if fire prevention, detection, automatic extinguishment and the restraints against the spread of fire are made more effective. This will mean that the private sector will have to assume more responsibility for fire prevention detection and early control.

Guards

In 1975, fewer than 500,000 people were employed full time or part time in security services. Today, that number is more than 1 million and growing. Security service work has become one of the fastest growing jobs in the United States.

Both proprietary and contract guard services are in greater demand than ever before, particularly for employment in hospitals and residential communities. Places that never even considered security are using guards today, said Barry Levy, president of B.W. Levy Associates of Chicago, a security consulting firm.

"The security industry as a whole is experiencing tremendous growth," he said. "As the economy worsens and crimes against individuals increase, companies are being forced to protect their employees and clients. As a result, people are turning more to guards because psychologically they may feel that hardware and technology may not offer enough protection."

Research by *Security World* tends to corroborate this increase. In a survey of security directors (December, 1980), about 58 percent of the respondents said they expected the use of contract guard services to increase in the next five years. About 61 percent said they expected the use of proprietary guards to increase over the same time period. In a separate survey of corporate executives (October, 1981), about 47 percent of the respondents said they expected their expenditures for guard services to increase in the next five years. More than 14 percent said the increase would be significant.

Major Trends

A major change in the guard industry, in both contract and proprietary sectors, will occur in terms of security guard supervision, Levy said. Because of the growing number of community colleges and universities offering security and law enforcement degrees, security management is becoming more professional.

19

Levy cited three basic trends that he anticipates to occur in the industry:

- As abuses or improper actions by guard personnel come to light, there will be more and louder cries by citizens and legislative bodies for tighter control and regulation of the industry. Although some groups may lobby against this, regulation of guards at the state level probably can be expected.
- As general unemployment rises, the security service industry will attract higher quality personnel.
- There will be a trend toward disarming the security personnel. Only certain supervisory personnel or guards in special, high risk situations will carry guns. This trend, which has already begun, is the result of increasing liability problems with armed guards. Banks, utilities, and other sensitive industry sectors may retain armed guards.

Contract vs. Proprietary

An ongoing debate in the industry has been the one on the relative merits of contract and proprietary security personnel. That debate is likely to continue.

Robert Johnson, president and general manager of First Security Services Corp. of Boston, a contract guard service company, sees a trend toward contract guard use.

"The service industry across the board is the fastest growing sector in the economy," Johnson said. "The modern security company is more than just a guard company. It offers management expertise and administrative convenience as well as flexibility for the client."

But some of the most significant changes in the guard industry are likely to occur on the proprietary side, Levy said.

"The contract and proprietary security guards serve different purposes," he said. "As time goes on, these differences may increase."

The contract and proprietary security guards serve different purposes," he said. "As time goes on, these differences may increase."

There is a trend in proprietary security, Levy said, for the guard to be better educated, have more responsibility, have more experience and receive a higher salary than his contract counterpart.

If this trend proves to be true, it may foster the development and use of a hybrid security staff composed of both contract and proprietary security personnel. Frontline security officers will be supplied by contract security companies for purposes of economics, training and readily available manpower. Proprietary security personnel will be used in supervisory and administrative roles for purposes of program continuity and familiarity with facilities.

In either case, however, training is likely to play an increasingly important role in the security service industry. Partly in response to state mandates for training, partly as a defense against liability for guard actions, and partly as a desire on the part of the guard company or client for better personnel, training is a part of the road to the future.

Once again, *Security World* surveys substantiate this trend. In a survey on security guard use (July, 1981) respondents ranked training for guard personnel as their third most important consideration in establishing a guard program, following only the reliability of guard personnel and the ability to tailor a program to specific needs. A survey of corporate executives (October, 1981) also indicated the likely growth of training programs. More than 35 percent of the respondents said that they expected funding for guard training programs to increase.

Economic Considerations

The general economic climate of the country will probably have the greatest impact on the use of guard services in the future. A fully proprietary guard force can be an expensive proposition for a business, and it may come to be an alternative that few companies are able to afford.

The general ill health of the economy, and the fact that companies are becoming increasingly careful of how and where they invest their operating capital, have fostered increased use of contract security services by many companies, said Joseph Cohen, director of consultant services for The

Kane Services of Chicago, a security service company. A well planned contract security program can be significantly less expensive than a proprietary force, he said.

On the line in day-to-day operations, the contract and proprietary security guard are not necessarily different, Cohen said. The difference is more often in the wants, desires and attitude of the corporate security director.

"Many security directors want to maintain their own little fiefdom with proprietary guards," he said. "Anything a propriet-ary security officer can do, a contract guard can do. But contract guards can be much lower in cost."

The trend toward contract security is also due to flexibility in expanding and cutting back guard forces as needed and to add liability protection, he said. Also, in some cases, contract guards are regulated, whereas proprietary are not.

On the balance, the future will see growth in the use of both electronic security equipment and security guard forces. The two elements of an effective security program will grow hand in hand, with the electronics increasing the surveillance and patrol capabilities of the guards, and the guards monitor-ing and responding to alarm conditions.

"Electronics don't think, guards do. Guards make the final determination on what to do in the event of an alarm," Cohen said. In the final analysis, that makes the difference between success and failure in a security program.

Training

The next decade will see increasing demands for improved personal performance on the part of both security profession-als and line security officers. That same demand for excellence is likely to increase the availability and scope of security education programs.

Whether for the line security officer or for the administra-tively oriented security director, whether in the structure of a university or the practical working environment, more oppor-tunities for security education and training will be available to more individuals in the security industry than ever before.

To a certain extent, the proliferation of training programs

will reflect the concerns and expectations of the security industry itself. For example, in a *Security World* survey of security directors (December, 1980), 81 percent of the respondents said that they expect increases in corporate security training programs in the next five years. In another survey on the use of security guards (July 1981), security directors responding to the survey said that guard training programs were their third most important consideration in establishing a guard program, superseded only by the reliability to tailor a guard program to their specific needs.

Corporate executives apparently mirror the concern for training. In a survey on corporate attitudes toward security (October, 1981), more than 35 percent of the corporate executives answering the survey said that they expect to spend more money on guard training programs, and more than 68 percent said they expected to spend more money on employee security training programs.

What accounts for the growing concern for training? The answers are found in the same forces driving advances in security education in both the academic and business environment.

The Academic Environment

"People are security conscious today, and we're seeing more security programs being offered in colleges and universities, especially as courses in criminal justice programs. That trend is likely to continue," said Norman Bottom, president of the Academy of Security Educators and Trainers and associate professor in the department of criminology at Indiana University of Pennsylvania.

A change is also likely to occur within the nature of the security education programs themselves, Bottom said. The security practitioner will tend to become more business oriented, essentially being forced into a better understanding of business by modern management trends. And the trend toward business education may induce friction in the industry at large.

The educational environment will put pressure on the security industry, Bottom said, in terms of the increased expectations it generates in graduates of security programs. The new breed of business oriented security professionals may come into conflict with an older generation of security professionals who see security and business management as two separate functions.

There may also be some degree of friction in the academic environment itself. Traditionally, most security programs have been contained within the framework of a college's criminal justice program. But as business management becomes more a part of modern security administration, that may not be the best structure.

"Ideally, a security program should be contained in the school of business," Bottom said. "But business schools often have more than enough programs to occupy their time, or are too short sighted to consider developing a program. There may also be some reluctance on the part of the criminal justice programs to let security stand on its own or be a part of another department."

Despite those restraints, an increasing number of colleges and universities are establishing separate, free-standing programs in security administration. But this trend may slow in the immediate future, subjected to the pitfalls of the economy and cutbacks in state and federal funding to education.

"The single most important issue facing security education in the coming decade will be making peace with other educators in the criminal justice field," Bottom said. "Security is related to, but not identical with criminal justice, and that fact has to be established."

Another problem security will have to face, he said, is the fact that there is no formal security institution in the country. Security certification exists, but the certification is not comparable to that found for a doctor, an architect, an engineer or an attorney.

To help change that situation, Bottom said ASET was examining the possibility of creating some form of security institute within the next three years, with part of its efforts directed at formalizing the security industry.

Institutionalizing Security

But formalizing security at the academic level will only be a part of industry efforts in the next decade. Another major educational effort was initiated in Chicago in November, 1981, with the formal announcement of the Private Security Institute (PSI).

Organized as a private corporation, PSI is owned by a group of private security and criminal justice officials. Its efforts will be to provide ongoing training for both line and supervisory personnel.

"One of the problems of ongoing security education and training is that the training programs are here today and gone tomorrow," said Michael O'Mara, PSI president. "We'll be addressing that problem with a permanent training program for line security personnel available for 46 weeks during the year. Specialized training for security supervisors and directors and other company personnel will be available on an ongoing basis as needs dictate." Another part of the institute's activity will be in defining the roles and relationship of private security and law enforcement.

The traditional role of security has been to prevent crime, O'Mara said. The traditional role of law enforcement has been to react to crime. As such, the two are at opposite ends of the criminal justice spectrum. But because the two deal with the same subject, O'Mara said that there is a need for greater cooperation between the public and the private sector.

"The Law Enforcement Assistance Administration and the various programs it had to help local law enforcement are effectively dead," he said."The days of big budgets for law enforcement departments are also over. But business and private citizens are going to expect the level of service they are familiar with to continue. That's where private security comes in. Security can work effectively with law enforcement if it knows how."

Accordingly, the institute will offer training in public/private security cooperation in both its basic course for line security personnel and in an advanced specialized course entitled

"Techniques for Developing a Coalition Between the Police and Private Security Forces."

The cooperation can come at several levels, O'Mara said. At its simplest, it could be common communications channels on police and private security radios, or help in crowd control or the preservation of evidence at the scene of a crime. On a more complex level, it can be a better understanding of the legal limitations defining the roles of private security and police.

"The point is that there has been no ongoing mechanism to make this cooperation possible," O'Mara said. "We can fill that vacuum with our training programs, and the training can be standardized to make it effective over a broad area."

Formal training starts at the PSI's facility in Itasca, a suburb of Chicago, in January of 1982. A satellite facility will begin operation in Los Angeles in February, followed by a New York City satellite facility in April. As many as 26 different courses could be offered in 1982, depending on industry response. Additional specialized courses will be developed as responses dictate, including one course currently in development on general security administration. Intended for department directors, the course could be completed in nine months of full time attendance, or in three years with night class attendance on a part time basis.

"The major impact of the institute will be that it provides a permanence and accountability in security education and training, and that it will provide training in a practical, real-world situation," O'Mara said. "It will establish a level of quality and a standardization that doesn't exist in the industry at this time."

That improved standard of quality, both for line and administrative security personnel, will go a long way in helping security meet the increasing legal and professional demands that will be placed on it in the coming decade.

Computer Crime

Just as it has in the past decade, the use of computers in the 1980s will continue to revolutionize the way in which business is conducted. The computers will also revolutionize some of the traditional views on what security threats are important to a company.

As more general company data and tactical management data are stored in computers, and as more transfers of funds and assets take place by way of the computer, the computer itself can become the lifeblood of a company. Alteration or destruction of the data or the computer system, or even simple errors in the use of the data or the system, can have disasterous effects on a business' ability to continue operations. As such, computers can be, and are likely to become, the most important focus for a corporate security program.

This type of evolution should come as no surprise to security professionals. In a survey of security directors (December, 1980) about 88 percent of the respondents said they expect increased activity in terms of computer crime for the next five years. About 49 percent of the respondents said the increase would be significant.

Why are the risks for computers increasing? In a story in its April 20, 1981, edition, *Business Week* magazine cited several reasons. More employees have access to computer terminals as they appear in increasing numbers in the office environment; more students are learning how to use computers and are becoming sophisticated enough to learn how to outwit computer security; and more consumers are using personal computers. About 500,000 are in use today, and the number is expected to increase to about 3 million by the middle of the decade.

Another reason not included in the story is opportunity. According to various industry sources, about $400 billion in funds are transferred on an electronic basis per day in the United States. Similarly, about $600 billion are transferred per day on an international level. The sheer volume alone provides an opportunity for losses due to error or fraud.

Some estimates put the toll of reported and unreported computer crime at more than $3 billion annually. The FBI reports that the typical take for a reported crime is about $500,000. This is substantially higher than the $3,000 reported for the typical bank robbery, and the $23,000 reported for the typical incident of embezzlement.

Difficult Definitions

"You have to be careful in reporting the numbers for computer crime, because there is no valid mechanical or statistical method of accounting for them," said Donn Parker of SRI International of Menlo Park, Calif. Parker is one of the nation's leading authorities on the topic of computer crime. "Even the figures reported by the FBI can be open to debate."

In understanding the losses that can be incurred through a computer system, it is also important to differentiate losses due to unintentional errors from intentional acts on the part of systems operators.

"The security problem in data processing has not been and will not be dishonesty. It is simple errors in data entry. This can be very disruptive to a business, especially in a large corporation with many computer terminals," said Robert Courtney Jr. of Robert Courtney Inc., an independent security consultant specializing in risk assessment, contingency planning and other high technology aspects of data security.

Assessing the threats or losses a computer operation faced, Courtney said they can be ranked according to the danger they posed to a company. In descending order, Courtney said the threats have ranked, and will continue to rank, as follows:

1. Errors and omissions in data entry: as much as 80 percent of computer losses could be accounted for by this.
2. Dishonest employees: these are clerks and other operations personnel who use a computer system with an intent to defraud.
3. Uncontrollable acts or events: these would include floods, fires, riots, accidents or other unpredictable events.
4. Disgruntled employees: this is an employee who wants to cause loss or damage to a company, but has no economic motive of his own. These incidents are relatively few in number, but often high in the dollar value of the damage.
5. Water damage not related to floods or fires: the most common example of this would be leaking plumbing or sprinkler systems.
6. Vandals, dissidents, terrorists or other non-company personnel intent on causing damage to a computer system.

"Physical assaults happen on computers, but they are relatively few in numbers," Courtney said. "More often than not, the data or the program is the target.

"You also have to realize that computer crime is not growing on its own. It is growing in proportion to the growth of computer systems use in general. The real key to controlling system losses is to hold the people using them accountable and responsible for their actions."

Threats at the High End

Although simple errors and omissions will continue to be a major concern for computer security, the skilled computer criminal is likely to merit more concern in the future.

"We'll see a more sophisticated computer criminal in the future," Parker said. "We're starting to see more of this now on a case by case basis of large losses. Large scale and large level fraud will be more prevalent in the future, even if the media does not report a large number of these cases."

Although many of these sophisticated criminals will be company employees, Parker said there may also be a movement of the career criminal into computer theft and fraud. Organized crime may also get involved in the use of computers for theft or fraud, or in the theft of computer data itself.

Fortunately, the picture is not entirely pessimistic," Parker said. "As computer vulnerability grows, so does the concern for protecting the computers, the data and the operating processes. We've already seen the growth and development of data encryption and operating software as a means to control computer crime, and this development is likely to increase in the future. The use of front end security measures such as identification and verification devices will probably increase in the future, as will the use of various forms of security hardware to fortify buildings and data processing areas.

"The use of electronic data processing auditors is also likely to increase with time. As long as computing systems remain vulnerable, there will be the motivation to safeguard them."

A Weakness Within Growth

One major problem computer security will face in the coming years is the growth of distributed data processing and the inherent lack of data integrity that it fosters.

As data passes between remote terminals and central computer units, by means of telecommunications, there is a danger that the data can be intercepted or altered. Data encryption can help in making intercepted data useless to anyone lacking a compatible decrypting device, a source in the federal sector said, but care must be taken to supervise the telecommunications path to prevent intrusion, data alteration and the opportunity for data interception.

Another major problem will be encountered in the increasing dependence of business and industry on the computer as a essential tool for day-to-day business operations.

"The chances of physical damage to a computer are slim, but the consequences of that damage assumes major proportions when its impact on business is considered," said Cameron Carey, data processing manager for the Computer Security Institute.

"Organizations are starting to worry more and more about what could happen if their computer hardware was suddenly gone. With the amount of business transacted by computers on a daily basis, losses could easily total into the millions for some companies. Some have even estimated they could cease to function as a business in a matter of days without computer support."

The gravity of this point is driven home by information in the Sark Report issued in Sweden. According to Parker, the report stated computers were an issue of national security in Sweden, and that Sweden could effectively cease to function as a country if it lost its computer capabilities to any great extent.

Various companies have responded to this type of threat, Carey said, by establishing "empty shell" facilities and disaster recovery units. These are facilities and back-up equipment that can be brought on line in the event of any major damage to a primary computer system.

A Lack of Laws

It might be expected that the growth of computer crime would foster the growth of a body of law to help control it. Some laws have been written to change the criminal code and update it to the changing nature of crime, Parker said, but only about 15 states have put computer crime statutes on their books to date.

Why haven't the laws kept pace with the problem? "Some bills have been penned, but they've died in committees because of perceived lack of need or of unsuitability to the crime," said Fred Greguras of Omaha, Neb., an attorney specializing in high technology legal issues. "Some existing laws could cover some of the crimes, but many judges and prosecutors are not familiar with how a computer operates. Apart from that, there is still a debate on just how the computer criminal should be identified and defined.

"But legal systems would benefit from some form of specific legislation on computer crime. Prosecutors would have something specific to peg their efforts into."

But apart from reaction after the fact, legal issues are likely to promote preventive security efforts for computers because of liability problems. "Liability will come into play in the future as a basic concern of business activity," Greguras said. "The computer has become the lifeline of a company and its functions. Because it has become so important, it has to be secured. There will be an increasing chance that a company, in the event of a problem, will be held liable for failing to take the necessary steps to provide for computer protection."

White Collar Crime

Internal theft has always been a security problem for business and industry, and the problem is likely to continue in the future.

In the past, the employee pilferage component of internal theft has generally presented more of a problem than the white collar crime component. And while employee theft is likely to remain a major concern for retailers and distribution chains, the white collar crime problem is likely to merit increasing attention from many large businesses and industries in the coming years.

Both types of crimes rank high among executive concerns about security. In a *Security World* survey of corporate attitudes, (October, 1981), respondents indicated that employee pilferage and white collar crime ranked fourth and fifth among the major security threats facing business, following only theft of funds and theft of property in the ranking. In an earlier survey of security directors (December, 1980), 89 percent of the respondents said that they expect white collar crime to increase in the next five years. About 50 percent of the respondents said the increase would be significant.

A Democratic Crime

What is happening to white collar crime to make it more of a concern to security programs? The answer is found in the changing nature of business. White collar job functions are moving down the corporate ladder, thanks primarily to the use of computers in a wider range of business activities.

"The impact of the computer has been to democratize white collar crime," said Robert Courtney Jr., of Robert Courtney, Inc., an independent security consultant specializing in risk assessment, contingency planning and high technology aspects of data security.

"Jobs that used to be in the province of senior management people are now being done by lower level personnel who are familiar with the use of computer terminals. There used to be a separation of financial duties as well. Now those duties are becoming more centralized to a single computer operator and his terminal. The problem is that there is generally a lack of checks an balances to keep the lower level personnel from taking funds from the company."

The lack of adequate safeguards for the problem, Courtney said, may be due to a misconception of what white collar crime constitutes today. There is no real proof that there will be an increase of traditional white collar crimes such as the embezzlement of funds by a major corporate officer, he said, but a trend does exist to indicate that an increasing number of computer related white collar crimes will take place in the future.

The scope of white collar crime becomes apparent when it is considered in its relationship to computer crime. "White collar crime is not necessarily synonymous with computer crime," said Donn Parker, a security management systems consultant with SRI International in Menlo park, Calif. "Realistically, a computer can be involved in any type of crime there is.

"But about 80 to 90 percent of the computer crime that takes place is a type of white collar crime. And the increased use of computers is democratizing white collar crime and making it worse."

Current estimates on dollar losses in computer crimes run from a low of $100 million to as much as $3 billion. The estimates are tenuous, however, because many of the computer crimes are never detected or reported.

Protecting Against Internal Threat

Defenses against the white collar computer criminal are difficult to develop, partly because of the nature of the criminal himself. The systems operator has a legitimate reason for access to, and use of, the system as a part of his job. Accordingly, hardware devices such as access controls or personal identification and authorization systems may not deter the operator from theft.

To defend against this type of computer criminal is to defend against the alteration or addition of computer data while the system is in operation. A number of software programs are available to do this. The software programs are an integral part of the computer programming itself, and can limit or prohibit an operators ability to add, subtract or alter data in the system. Used with adequate access, identification and authorization devices, and identification codes, this type of security application can go a long way in reducing internal computer theft. An increasing number of computer systems are likely to use this type of device in the future.

Another key to deterring this type of white collar crime is detecting it and controlling the opportunity for it. To that end, external electrical data processing auditors have played, and will continue to play, a role in controlling white collar computer crime. Just as traditional auditors have uncovered irregularities in a company's records, so can the data auditors uncover irregularities in a company's data processing.

"External auditors are likely to become more important in the future," said Cameron Cary, data processing manager for the Computer Security Institute. "The only problem is that they often feel they should not make suggestions for more effective computer controls because they must be free to objectively assess the controls in place. Those controls are usually formulated by the data user organization or company."

Ethics and Values

The ultimate defense against the computer white collar criminal will have to take place at the personal level, in terms of the individuals operating the system and their supervisors. According to Parker, companies must foster a feeling of ethics and responsibility at the same time they are making more concrete efforts to provide security. Unfortunately, there is no guarantee that this people-oriented approach will work.

"We have no indication at all in our society today to suggest that employees or management will adopt corporate goals as a part of their own goals," said independent security consultant Charles Sennewald of Huntington Beach, Calif. "In fact, there are times when you see the opposite.

"White collar criminals have become more sophisticated, and they are likely to continue to do so. They'll be sophisticated in using the technology of doing business, and in doing business itself. And that will place more demands on the corporate security director. He'll have to be a businessman first, and a security man second."

"I'd predict that internal security staffs are likely to get more involved in the investigation, reporting and prosecution of white collar crime," said Kirk Barefoot, director of risk management for Cluett, Peabody & Co. of New York, a large clothing manufacturing and sales company.

"This is not necessarily tied into an increase in white collar crime as much as it is to new business awareness and practices. Businesses are getting the idea that if they are going to get their maximum dollar profit, they're going to have to squeeze as much as they can out of their security departments. They're also going to have to cut their losses as much as possible."

Public law enforcement has helped in the past and will probably continue to help in the future, but reduced law enforcement funding may force police departments to set priorities on the services they offer. Internal theft problems may not be high on that list, so more investigative responsibility will be placed on the security department.

But cooperation will still exist between the public and private sectors. There is a definite trend, Barefoot said, for companies to work with the criminal justice system in prosecuting employees involved in wrongdoing. This trend is likely to continue and become more of a formal policy as business, and specifically top management, becomes more security conscious.

"After all," he said, "it's the man at the top who has to set the policy and the moral tone of the company."

Liability & Insurance

In the past, the courts have generally maintained a hands-off attitude toward private security matters. But as the size and scope of private security has increased, so has its exposure to liability. And litigation resulting from that increased exposure is on the rise as well.

The security director's hiring, training and firing procedures, in particular, are more open to legal action than ever before.

Background checks are increasing in importance as liability in the hiring process increases, said David Steeno, attorney and assistant professor in law enforcement, Western Illinois University. For example, if an unfit employee is placed in a position where that employee can hurt someone, the firm may be open to charges of negligent hiring if a problem arises. Arming a security guard is an instance of where an employer's responsibility for hiring a stable, qualified individual assumes major importance. But security faces another problem in this case. Privacy legislation has made the task of background checks a difficult one for security departments to do adequately, even though the procedure is becoming more important.

After an employee has been hired, the employer assumes responsibilities for his work-related actions. In the case of a security guard, if he is not properly trained, the employer may be held liable for any wrongdoing by the guard. This dilemma of arming security guards has caused many employers to weigh the benefits of having armed security personnel. An agency that arms their guards is at a much greater exposure to liability, Steeno said.

Even a firm that uses guards from a contract agency may not be immune to liability problems. Courts are currently examining the contractor relationship to liability. Conceivably, a company hiring a guard agency could be held liable in its selection of that agency under some doctrine of comparative or third-party liability.

Document All Violations

One area of growing sensitivity involves employee termination without sufficient cause. "An employee who is terminable at-will can theoretically be fired for any reason as long as his civil rights are not violated," Steeno said. "But courts are starting to become more protective of the employee, and many want a reason for termination."

Because of this trend in the courts, one employee who was fired because she was suspected of theft — a suspicion upheld by a polygraph examination that she consented to — was able to successfully sue the company of defamation because of the accusation.

These types of rulings will make it more important than ever for security departments to document all company policy violations thoroughly and carefully — even if they include such minor incidents as exiting from the wrong door.

Professional Risks

"As security managers place themselves among the ranks of other professionals by instituting industry certification or degrees and other means, they will be held to a higher standard of expectation than the layman, and in the future they will be held accountable for their actions," said Robert F. Johnson, president, First Security Services Corp., Boston. As a result, the issue of malpractice is likely to be applied to the security industry in the '80s, he said.

Today's and tomorrow's security manager is responsible for protecting millions of dollars of a company's assets. If he represents himself as a security expert, certain standards that represent that skill will be expected of him. It will be important, therefore, for the security manager to be careful not to raise the level of expectation too high. He must recognize and disclose, upfront, what he believes security can and cannot accomplish. "If we continue to raise unreasonable expectations, someone will turn around and call us on it," Johnson said.

Vulnerability Varies

Certain areas of private security are more vulnerable than others. The retail sector, probably the most exposed, has been experiencing a marked increase in litigation in recent years, particularly involving store detectives charged with false arrests and malicious prosecution. This increase is attributable to the security departments' high degree of public contact. Add to that public contact an aggressive security force, and the equation equals greater exposure to legal entanglements, particularly in the area of civil or criminal liability.

Hospitals and hotels also must contend with high public contact, but they have not had the same amount of problems as retail security. Lack of public contact in industrial security and other more isolated security specialities also make them less vulnerable to liable suits.

Insuring the Risk

As a firm's vulnerability to liability and other security-related losses grows, it may consider insurance as a vehicle for assuming more risks.

Crime insurance covering employee dishonesty, forgery, and loss of valuables due to theft and fire has been available for many years. But, within the past 10 years, the claims and frequency of employee dishonesty have skyrocketed, and large companies have for the first time begun to seek out policies covering losses from employee theft. What was once a minor part of a company's insurance portfolio has become a large part of its coverage.

A major, and growing, area in employee dishonesty insurance is fidelity liability insurance. This coverage is designed for companies whose employees have access to the property of others. If an employee steals from a client, for example, the company would be covered for that liability. Temporary help agencies and management consultants are examples of this type of policy holder.

Crime is a major factor spurring these changes. The rising crime rate has become foremost in public and business thinking; they are concerned about protecting what they have. Part of the change is undoubtedly due to the changing attitude of the white collar worker. He sees other people steal, or he feels the effects of inflation. In many cases temptation, in the form of a computer, is at his fingertips.

Policy of the '80s.

The advent of electronic data processing has opened up entire new areas for major losses to business. An individual with a little knowledge of data processing and one computer terminal can steal millions in cash, goods or services from a company and go undetected for years.

"The insurance industry is trying to come to grips with modern technology," said Christopher Barr, assistant vice president, American Home/National Union Insurance Companies, a division of American International Group. "Computer insurance may be the policy of the '80s," he said. Right now, computer theft insurance, called computer and funds transfer insurance by AIG, is still a new type of coverage and only offered by a few firms.

Insurance Evolution

"The next few years will see a substantial change in the crime insurance policy. There will be an evolution of insurance to cover existing needs. Companies will no longer say we have four crime policies available. They already recognize that it's a whole new area of insurance and policies will be tailor-made; it will be more of a consumer approach," Barr said.

Sensitive Risk

Companies who do business overseas are turning to the insurance industry to protect their investments. They are buying policies not only to cover their executives in the event of kidnapping, but they are also insuring against actions of foreign governments, including coverage for employee evacuations as well as for nationalization of industries.

This type of sensitive risk insurance is expected to become more prevalent in the future, not just because the problems are increasing, but partly because as insurance companies become more sophisticated and meet the customers' needs more precisely, more people consider insurance a viable means of financial protection.

Insurance & Industry

The potential for the insurance industry to influence security standards is great. However, insurance is a competitive industry, and the likelihood of it forcing new standards of industry security in today's economy is unlikely. At the moment insurance companies are taking a more passive role by recommending security to their clients. However, chances are good that in the future, insurance companies will influence commercial standards of security to some extent.

Screening

When it comes to employee screening and testing, the security industry is likely to find itself between the proverbial "rock and a hard place" in the next few years. A demand will exist for more careful screening and selection of employees, but it may be difficult to satisfy that demand in light of privacy legislation and a strict legal limits on the extent to which an inquiry about an individual can be made.

In simple terms, a company can face a suit from an individual for invasion of privacy if its investigation goes too far. Conversely, the company can suffer the damages of a liable suit if the employee causes some sort of job related injury to a third party, and it can be proven that the company's investigation of the employee was not thorough enough.

There's no perfect solution to the problem, but there is help for it by means of employee screening.

Traditionally, screening has been done using either a polygraph test or some form of paper-and-pencil testing. But over the years about 20 states have developed legislation restricting the use of polygraphs. Numerous laws exist prohibiting a polygraph test as a condition of employment.

In answer to these restrictions and the still apparent need for screening, there has been a trend toward the increasing use of paper-and-pencil testing of prospective employees. Polygraph tests are still being used and will continue to be used for investigations and the hiring of some personnel for sensitive positions, particularly those relating to national security. But in the private sector, paper test will increasingly come into the spotlight.

"Companies are getting tired of being robbed by their own employees, and they want a way to screen out the dishonest employee before he comes into a company," said Doug Wicklander, national sales manager of The Reid Report, of Chicago, a firm that conducts pre-employment and paper-and-pencil tests. "They've spent a tremendous amount of dollars trying to keep burglars out and trying to solve thefts internal to the company. Now they're starting to try and control the problem on the front end by trying to keep dishonest employees out in the first place."

A Viable Alternative

Although the paper-and-pencil approach to honesty testing has been around since the early 1950s, its widespread use has grown relatively recently. Apart from restrictive state legislation on polygraph testing, Wicklander said other factors have contributed to its growth.

In many cases, he said, companies cannot justify the cost for polygraph or psychological stress evaluator testing when a paper-and-pencil test can achieve the needed results for less money. Business and industry in general have also experienced the growth of chain or franchise locations. Without a central location to process all employees, there can be a problem in the consistency or standardization of the polygraph tests. The paper-and-pencil test can be taken at any location and mailed to a central location for standardized processing.

"The paper-and-pencil tests have an accuracy of about 86 to 88 percent," he said. "The biggest difference between the tests and a polygraph is that the polygraph gives an indication of the truth with respect to the past actions of the individual being tested. The paper-and-pencil tests can determine the attitudes of the individual toward honesty and indicate whether he thinks like a person who would or would not steal."

A Legal Alternative

A major strength of the trend toward paper-and-pencil honesty testing is the fact that it avoids legal problems that can be tied into polygraphs or psychological stress evaluators. An attempt to prohibit the honesty test was made in the Minnesota anti-polygraphing law, but that attempt was later overturned by the Minnesota Supreme Court.

"There are no major state restrictions on honesty testing as a form of pre-employment screening," said Carl Klump, president of the Stanton Corp., of Chicago, another firm active in paper-and-pencil pre-employment testing and screening. "It is generally viewed as just another form of pre-employment testing. Even the unions have not objected to it.

"That is not to say, however, that there may not be objections to it at some time in the future. As this testing approach becomes more common, there may be some reaction to it. The Minnesota law was an example of this. But there's no way to predict what will follow."

Expanded Applications

"Screening enjoys different levels of acceptance across the country, but I think the growth of paper-and-pencil testing will be active in the future," said Charles Sennewald, an independent security consultant from Huntington Beach, Calif. "Few security organizations will not have testing as a part of staff screening.

"Philosophically, I think that some form of screening is one of the best things that a security department can do. Screening can be one of the best ways that a security department can avoid or respond to a liability problem, particularly in light of the legal limits on what can be done in terms of an inquiry into an employee's past.

"This liability application should be particularly important to top management. If a company brings in a shoddy employee, that company can, and often is, held responsible for the actions of that employee."

The savings afforded by avoiding liability suits can be substantial when they reached $10,000. Today, jury awards of more than $100,000 are a common event, and awards in excess of $800,000 are not unheard of.

Apart from this type of front end security, both in terms of selecting reliable employees and reducing exposure to liability, both Wicklander and Klump agree that paper-and-pencil tests will gain wider use for evaluating and testing employees already on the payroll, or in conducting internal investigations.

A variation of the test can be given, Wicklander said, to evaluate an individual's planned promotion into a more responsible or sensitive company position. Another variation of the test can be given on a case by case basis for the investigation of an internal theft, Klump said, with accuracy of 80 to 85 percent. This type of test would refer to the specific incident under investigation.

Apart from this individual case review, future research and development of paper-and-pencil tests will make them applicable to measure employee attitudes on absenteeism, productivity, drug use and other topics that can affect a company, and an employee's relations with a company.

"The tests have developed rapidly since their conception, and there's no end in sight for further development," Klump said. "In five to ten years, the amount of information that will be able to be developed using the tests will be amazing."

Executive Protection

The primary security concerns of corporate executives are the protection of funds and property, according to an October, 1981, *Security World* survey. But another concern is attracting growing attention from this group, particularly among those whose firms operate internationally. That concern is for the protection of people.

More than 50 percent of the executives responding to the survey said that their company already had an executive protection program or felt that their company should have an executive protection program.

Most of them realize that although the chances of an attack on one of their executives is not nearly as likely or predictable as employee theft, one kidnap incident could cost the company more than five years of losses due to internal theft.

The loss of a key executive can be a critical event for a company, in terms of its own operation or in terms of liability. Precedent has been set in several cases for kidnap victims or their families to file suit against a company on the grounds that security precautions were inadequate or that response to the kidnapping and following negotiations were too slow. On the other hand, precedent has also been set for stockholders to file suit against a company for responding to kidnap demands at the expense of company profits.

How damaging can these situations be? In the past 10 years an estimated $300 million in ransom has been paid in political kidnappings, according to Risks International, a Washington D.C.-based firm that provides information to businesses on political terrorism. And, as of late, it is not unusual for a ransom demand for one executive to exceed $10 million.

The number of executives kidnapped, and the ransom amounts paid, cannot be pinned down because most companies keep these incidents quiet, even after a demand has been paid and the individual has been safely returned. Many companies believe that releasing this information will increase their vulnerability to more terrorist activities.

Why White Collar Targets?

A predominant factor influencing the increase in threats to individuals relates directly to the increase in threats to business.

The business executive is a surrogate target, especially if he is viewed to represent Western power and wealth. Whether he's the chairman of the board or one of many plant managers, as a surrogate target he runs the same risks as his employer.

Statistics bear this risk relationship out. In recent years there has been an upswing in the number of threats against business — particularly in the areas of kidnappings and bombings. In 1980, there were 124 reported kidnappings, 57 of them involved businessmen. "Businessmen are ideal kidnap targets because companies almost always pay the ransom demanded. As one European terrorist stated several years ago, ransoms paid for kidnapped businessmen are a primary source of operating capital for most terrorist groups," according to a report from Risks International.

Kidnappings and bombings are likely to remain favored tactics because both rely heavily on the fact that neither businesses nor businessmen can isolate themselves from the public. They must be open to public contact.

Some businessmen are obviously more vulnerable than others. The executive who runs the gretest risk is likely to be part of an organization with high visibility, a great deal of foreign exposure, political connotations such as an oil company or a weapons manufacturer, or a company that is known to have paid kidnap ransoms in the past.

"Concern over specific issues such as nuclear energy, pollution and abortion could lead to the use of terrorist tactics. Even reaction against high technology has provoked violence," said Brian Jenkins, research analyst with the Rand Corporation and an authority on international terrorist activities and trends.

What's Likely to Happen

Based on an analysis of terrorist targeting from 1970 to 1980, Risks International estimates that in the 1980s, one-third of all terrorist operations will affect business, making it the largest single category affected by terrorist groups worldwide. An upswing in the targeting of U.S. firms in 1980 is a trend that is expected to continue.

This question of safety for the company and its people may influence business investments abroad. Many companies presently employ in-house risk analysts or use outside specialists for political as well as economic information on countries they are considering investing in.

"Political risk assessment is growing. It's becoming fashionable," said Hilliard Zola, president of International Consulting Group, which specializes in risk assessment, international business intelligence and personal security. Zola's firm is concerned with the protection and preparation of exposed executives. As political risk assessors, ICG examines the client company's profile and location and identifies the risks that the executive faces. At this point, they prepare a written response plan to implement in the event of a kidnapping and they help the client company form a crisis management team.

Business' concern with sensitive risks has also been felt by the insurance industry, and a new breed of coverage has evolved out of demand: kidnap, ransom and extortion insurance. The 1970s saw such a dramatic growth in domestic extortion and kidnappings in South America, that a few companies developed a specific policy. All indications are that because these risks will increase, so will insurance coverage of them.

The growing threat of terrorism has already effected some major trends in security. According to Brian Jenkins:

- Governments and the private sector have had to devote increasing attention and resources to internal security.
- The private security industry has grown tremendously and businesses have invested increasing amounts of money in security hardware and services.
- There has been a shifting of financial responsibilities for security and the private sector is taking a growing amount of responsibility for protection agains terrorism.
- A proliferation of "inner perimeters" has taken place. These are the rings of surveillance and protection that encircle airports, governments buildings and corporate headquarters.

Tomorrow's Terrorism

"Terrorism is likely to persist in the 1980s as a mode of political expression, of gaining international attention and of achieving limited political goals," Jenkins said. "Political violence in the United States will, for the near future, probably in some way mirror developments abroad, particularly the political struggles in Central America, the Caribbean and the Middle East."

Jenkins says that for the short-term, violence on behalf of Puerto Rican statehood may increase. For the long run, he points to some developments that may lead to events that contribute to terrorist activities.

- A rebirth of racism and growth of membership in racist groups.
- A resurgence of religious fanaticism that results in the proliferation of cults.
- A growing contempt toward the criminal justice system.
- An increase of narrow interest groups and single issue politics.
- An unmeasured decline in police intelligence activities.
- A growing mistrust of government and corporations as incompetent, negligent and irresponsible in protecting public health and safety.

- A sense of insecurity as a result of a growing perception that law enforcement cannot effectively protect citizens.

Where will the terrorist groups of the future come from? Most of the currently active groups show no sign of abandoning their cause, and it is possible that some of the groups lying dormant since the 1960s in the United States will reorganize to champion other causes.

In terms of the number of terrorist incidents, the United States is third among those countries experiencing the most terrorism. One of the reasons the problem is hardly noticed here is due to the unspectacular character of most incidents. Another reason is because the high level or ordinary crimes overshadows the relatively few terrorist attempts aimed at business.

2

The Security Profession
of the Future

Louis A. Tyska, CPP

I feel quite certain that when we reach the year 2000, we will be able to see the fruits of our planning of the eighties which will certainly have elevated our professional status to the heights for which we dreamed.

GEORGE C. MOORE, CPP

The most frightening question asked of oneself by a young person when growing up applies to us in the security profession at this time. Since no one really knows, we can each of us speculate and each are entitled to our own opinion. What follows is the future in the security profession as I see it.

In a word - Positive! Our profession is currently where the data processing pioneers were in the early to mid nineteen-sixties. We are at the dawn of a new and exciting role as a part of the business management team of the 21st Century. Every year more and more of the "Fortune One Thousand" companies worldwide recognize the need for a professional asset protection manager on their corporate staffs. This applies to positions in key regions, locations or countries. The position is called upon to advise and counsel managers on an ever increasing variety of subjects and this prediction for a rosey future can be made in confidence in spite of the fact that far too many of the world's top companies still remain without a professional in place.

As practioners in our discipline become increasingly more professional, competent and skilled, we collectively become more confident as well and hence begin to assert ourselves more and more in the battleground of management - the board room. The ability to communicate effectively along with the knowledge of the primary business philosophies of our various employers are essential parts of our preparation if we are to be accepted as a contributing staff profession. It is an acknowledged fact that security practioners generally maintain that "management" does not understand them. What is essentially true is that security people have communicated within their own circles, not upward and outward. In short, we have been talking to ourselves. *Obtaining acceptance and credibility has to be earned by each individual with what it is we each bring into the arena.* In any event, the general acceptance on the part of management representatives with whom we engage will dependent upon the rationality of our comments and presentations and our ability to effectively communicate. Therefore, we will need to "package" our recommendations into the kind and type of high level management presentations which demonstrates the professionalism we collectively are striving to obtain. We must utilize all of the techniques and apply them as appropriate to the unique demands of security. Our goals throughout all our communicative encounters with management must be toward relating to profit protection. Wherever and whenever possible, we must emphasize profitability through reduction of claims and actual loss, increased operational or service efficiency brought about by security related controls and by actual recoveries. In certain instances, emphasis needs to be placed on the need for the safety and security of top executives. There will be an increasing demand to verbally express the need to consider the security and asset protection perspectives when interfacing with varied management interests at least through the 90's, for ours is still an emerging profession and management needs to be convinced. We know from past experience that management deals with such needs as a tag on or lower priority in preparation and planning meetings, if at all. It is to this point that the security professional must accept the role of sales person with the main idea to foster whenever and wherever possible the need for understanding of and, at the very least, a sense of awareness about security concerns. This is best accomplished when a situation presents itself which needs clarification, emphasis or simply to point out potential problems. These types of opportunities generally present themselves at or during the endless process of management meetings. The security professional who can articulate in an effective, clear and concise manner will be listened to.

The selling job, which all of us who strive to elevate the security profession engage in, requires verbal skills and professional presentations but these alone will not suffice to attain that goal if we, as individuals, fail to look the part. Logic tells us that how a person looks in appearance should not influence the degree of knowledge a person can provide. However, credibility is influenced by outward appearance so it behooves each of us to adopt the particular style of grooming and dress that the specific organizations cadre adopt. Along with this, there of course is the managememt peer pressure element which spreads out to our lives outside the umbrella of the organizational "family" and into our private lives. How we spend our time socially, where we live, are we participating community citizens, do we pay our bills on time, are all questions and items which impact on our credibility and eventual acceptance. It is not implied that this is a correct condition, it simply is a price we pioneers of the security profession must pay if such is our commitment.

Will it be enough for the security professional to just know his business? I think not, for part of our success is being measured on the perceived ability collectively of all the current security people in industry and government on our ability to deal with people. Many business people appear to be loosing touch with the pulse of the work force and its varied population. Just the very nature of management's specialized disciplines and/or the pressure of business decisions or perhaps a simple lack of social awareness or knowledge concerning ethnic backgrounds or age tends to make this so. This is not the case with the security professional, his is a discipline that is inexorably linked to and with people. The knowledge of people and how to deal with them dictates that security professionals will become more of a part of the management needs of the future.

Security personnel will, if you accept the above, inherit an ever expanding role as a buffer for management to deal with the real people who comprise both the white and blue collar segments of the work force. This will demand that a base of knowledge on the part of the practioner be developed over a broad spectrum of skills in a variety of functions and professions which will comprise the work force of the future. This will be necessary in order to access the vulnerabilities to asset loss to the business we serve as influenced by the work force. John Naisbitt in his best seller, *Megatrends*, published by Warner Books, advises us that "in 1979 the number one occupation in the United States, numerically, became clerk." The clerk category replaced laborer. Further, "the second largest classification after clerk is professional."[1] Mr. Naisbitt goes on to explain that this occurrence is all in keeping with the transformation of the U.S. from an industrial society to an information society. There is much to support this theory and we, in the security profession, must acknowledge at the very least, two points which signal change and shift in concerns. These are: 1) the level of sophistication of theft and conspiracies will rise, and 2) the change in global locations of industrial and manufacturing centers will impact the security professionals worldwide.

Expanding upon this theory, it appears that there is a reluctance on the part of most general operating management to exercise their authority over the work force when questions of honesty, integrity or morals are at issue. A variety of reasons surface as being the cause of this: absence of social awareness by the manager; lack of experience in dealing with confrontation situations; fear of reprisal or simply just not wanting to give up the benevolent boss image of "Mr. Nice Guy." It is into this vacuum that the security professional leaps with a natural tendency for people-oriented problem-solving and the preconcieved notion on the part of management in general that the security person is accustomed to dealing with people-related confrontation.

Just what will be the profile of the people that we security professionals will be dealing with? They will most assuredly be older, have longevity with their specific employer, more intelligent, have been raised in a society which has progressed rapidly through technology advancements and finally, a work force which functions with a high degree of stress. "We must learn to balance the material wonders of technology with the spiritual demands of our human nature," "The need for human touch."[2] We must not exclude the various types of private corruption which involves a particular firm itself. "Commercial bribery involving American firms also occurs overseas. Payments have been made to numerous foreign corporations and to foreign subsidiaries of American firms. In many instances, the payments are kept secret from foreign governments as well."[3] So it becomes a clearly challenging sandbox in which the security managers of the future will play. New skills will be required. There will be new problems to solve based upon the same common denominator - people. Security without the "big brother is watching" syndrome, security without the depriving or restricting of personal rights of employees, security without the "Gestapo" image . . . how to establish it, how to prepare for it, are challenges to be overcome by the security professionals of the future-based on the strengths and acquired knowledge of the past as well as learning from the future as we live it.

During the coming decades we can anticipate that the number of formally educated persons in the security field will steadily rise. This will be caused by the advancing of Security Management and Asset Protection curricula in colleges and universities (particularly in the U.S.), the decline of the public sector to absorb the new entrants into the law enforcement community, and finally because the high tech era will demand it. The fields of electronics, robotic manufacturing, economics, behavioral sciences, and international and labor law will lead in influencing the training and professional development of the security professional. We are not preparing for this need at a fast enough pace and should we fall short of demand for our services, we collectively will not be considered professionally responsible. This could slow the growth and acceptance of our profession by our own lack of understanding of the situation. We must not let this happen. We must continually upgrade our knowledge and skills.

1. John Naisbitt. *Megatrends* (New York: Warner Books, 1981), page 5.
2. John Naisbitt. *Megatrends* (New York: Warner Books), Introduction.
3. August Bequai. *White Collar Crime: A 20th Century Crisis,* (Lexington, MA, Lexington Books/D.C. Heath and Company), page 43.

3

Developing A Professional Image for the Future

George C. Moore, CPP

Program Director — Administration of Justice
Northern Virginia Community College
Woodbridge, Virginia

PROFESSIONAL adj. — the conduct, aims or qualities that characterize or mark a profession or a professional person.[1]

Does Security fit within the boundaries of this definition? Speaking strictly from a technical interpretation of this definition, the answer to this question will probably be a qualified "yes."

However, from a practical point of view, it is generally recognized that to be a professional, a specialized field should at least possess the following elements:

1. A common foundation of knowledge.
2. Conforming to a code of ethics.
3. A valid screening process of personnel prior to being admitted to the profession.
4. Dedication of members of the profession to professional activities.
5. Following a line of professional conduct consistent with the demands of the particular profession.

Utilizing this measuring device, again one could say that security does fit the definition of a profession. But, perhaps it is not so important to debate whether or not security is now a profession as it is to see what we must do to assure we not only keep pace with the changing times from a security standpoint, but that we provide the necessary educational foundation for our security personnel to competently fulfill management responsibilities in the coming years, such responsibilities becoming increasingly complex year by year. If we are successful in this regard, we will not have to ponder the question as to whether we are members of a legitimate profession - our actions will clearly depict this professionalism to others.

Assuming, that there is no question as to security's status as a profession, a brief look at the current status of the security industry reveals it to be a multibillion dollar a year business which is predicted to grow at a rate of 10 - 12 per cent per year in the coming years. Not only is it an industry which affects practically all aspects of our society, but it is also an industry which has faced, and continues to face, a number of substantial problems which seem to accompany fast growth. In our quest for a blueprint to enhance our professional posture as we head into the twenty-first century we have a golden opportunity in this exciting field to overcome our weaknesses through a process of problem identification, education and implementation of solid management tehcniques designed for the future.

The magnitude of the problems which have confronted this profession in the past is vividly portrayed by the following observations made by Arthur J. Bilek in 1977, in his book entitled, *Private Security - Standards and Goals - From the Official Private Security Task Force Report:*

> Dilemmas, distortions and half-truths confront the student of private security. Critical analysis of the field evokes far more questions than answers. Confusion and uncertainty cloud the decision-making process concerning the efficacy of alternate security options. Practices are defended and decried simultaneously. Despite a history almost as old as man, private security continues to function as anachronistically as if it had never met the test of time.[2]

Since 1977, when this statement was made, much has been done. Of primary significance has been the publishing of the National Report of the Task Force on Private Security, entitled, *Private Security.* This was a comprehensive study of the entire private security field. Weaknesses were identified and solutions recommended.

In professional development, education plays the key role and of all weaknesses cited by the Task Force Report, none were more glaring than those which were education-related. For example, some of the major deficiencies documented in this regard were:

1. Inferior personnel with a high turnover rate,
2. Training for private security minimal or non-existent,
3. Lack of a viable certification program to increase the professionalism of the industry,
4. Lack of advanced training for private security supervisory and managerial personnel,
5. Need to endow a state regulatory agency with authority and responsibility for overseeing and evaluating private security training activities,
6. Lack of courses on architectural design for crime prevention in education institutions offering architecture curriculum,
7. Security administrators handicapped in decision making roles because of appalling lack of a reliable research base,
8. The need for seminars and courses given by colleges and universities to meet the needs of private security personnel,
9. The total inadequacy of educational programs at the baccalaureate and graduate levels designed to prepare persons for private security employment,
10. The need for a national private security resource and research institute to act as a center and resource for research activities.

One consistent theme established throughout the Task Force Report is the need for education and training in the private security field.

It would appear that a logical response to the identification of the aforementioned weaknesses in educational requirements would have been a mutually sponsored effort by educational institutions and private industry to initiate suggested recommendations and innovations so badly needed to correct these significant deficiencies.

However, such has not been the case. In fact, *the future development of private security as a profession could be in real jeopardy unless steps are taken soon on an international basis to expedite meaningful educational programs designed to meet the current and future needs of the private security industry* which is still in a period of rapid and steady growth.

Bearing in mind the widespread educational deficiencies, it is actually a tribute to the American Society of Industrial Security (ASIS) with a membership of over 23,000 members (1985) that this industry has been making considerable progress as a profession.

A number of viable and effective measures have been instituted by ASIS and other professional organizations to provide their members and associates with educational resources.

Some examples of educational programs and assets afforded by ASIS for professional development purposes are:

1. The annual seminar, which in 1985 produced over 86 hours of educational programs,
2. Establishment of the two Security Programs which provide 5 day educational courses in Protection of Assets, Security Management and Review for Certification Examinations,
3. A wide variety of workshops and seminars on specialized subjects such as terrorism, guard management, behavorial science in law enforcement and security, hostage situations and survival skills, legal problems and the American business person abroad,
4. The Certified Protection Professional (CPP) Program,
5. The monthly publication, "Security Management,"
6. Sponsorship of scholarships and internships,
7. Publication of texts and pamphlets on specialized security subjects,
8. The granting of Continuing Educational Units(CEU's) for participation in educational programs,
9. Assistance provided to colleges and universities in instituting degree programs, as well as specialized seminars,
10. The maintenance of a library utilized for research

purposes.

11. Adoption of a Code of Ethics.

Of the above endeavors which have an impact on the private security industry from an educational standpoint, the one which deserves special mention is the CPP Program.

The purpose of the certification program are as follows:

1. To raise the professional standing for the field and improve the practice of security management by giving special recognition to those security practitioners who, by meeting prescribed standards of performance, knowledge and conduct have demonstrated a high level of competent and ethical practice.

2. To identify sources of professional knowledge of the principles and practices of security and loss prevention, related disciplines and of laws and regulations governing or affecting the practice of security.

3. To encourage security professions to carry out a continuing program of professional development.

This Certification Program has been quite successful and is probably the most singular development in the past decade in the promotion of professionalism in private security. Education, as it should, plays a very important role in this process. Prior to being elegible to take the written examination of 300 questions on twelve security disciplines, the applicant for the CPP Examination must meet specified experience and/or educational requirements. In addition, the successful applicants must be re-certified each three years. Such re-certification depends upon the accumulation of six professional credits during this three year period, most of which can be earned through participation in educational activities. Approximately 1,000 security professionals have been certified to date through this program's examination process.

Despite the impressive growth of the security industry and professional organizations such as the American Society for Industrial Security, educational growth in this profession has not kept pace with economic growth. In fact, *during the past several years,* security educational initiatives on the part of colleges and universities in the United States have been sluggish or non-existent.

Although weaknesses in security education at our academic institutions are substantial, these are identifiable and can be remedied if the security industry takes a leadership role and provides the necessary incentives which will result in security curriculum developments responsive to changing needs of industry and society as a whole.

Some of the major security educational training weaknesses in the United States are:

1. There are only approximately fifty institutions which offer 4 year degrees of some type in security. Many areas have absolutely no academic degree programs. In the Washington D.C. regional area for example, there is no four year institution which offers a degree in security or security-related matters.

2. There are less than fifteen educational institutions offering a Master's degree in security.

3. There are less than 150 colleges throughout the country offering credit courses in security and many of these do not offer degree programs.

4. Many institutions offering security courses do so in their Criminal Justice program areas to fill a void caused by the demise of the Law Enforcement Assistance Administration which provided considerable financial support to police science courses. As a result, security courses in many institutions are taught by faculty who lack basic qualifications and knowledge of private security foundation concepts. Likewise, the security curriculum in these colleges often are more police oriented in their design.

5. Textbooks in this field are still inadequate, although some of the publishers have recently recognized the need, especially in the introductory study areas and have published texts of good quality. There are major security disciplines in which there are few or no textbooks available.

6. There is a lack of planned direction for our security educational programs. In this regard there is no professional agreement as to either the format of such curricula on whether the focus should be along the lines of business management or criminal justice. Such lack of direction adds to existing confusion and certainly retards professional growth.

An analysis of the above weakness shows quite clearly

the immediate need for a sense of direction in all our security educational activities, not only to correct existing shortcomings, but more important, to develop a master plan which will lead us through this decade and into the year 2000 at least.

International Symposium Before the Year 2000

One of the first futuristic workshops was conducted by the editors of this book: Fennelly and Tyska, in 1984 at the ASIS annual seminar. The room was packed with people; some were standing out in the hall.

The time is right for an international symposium, of the highest intellectual and technical makeup available to the private security profession which will address the major security issues, both contemporary and futuristic and develop a pragmatic master plan, together with recommended procedures to guarantee implementation by the key societal components concerned. Ideally, such a symposium should be a joint endeavor of private security, academia and the public criminal justice sector. Because of previously stated reasons, this symposium should be organized and conducted solely by private security under the auspices of ASIS which is really the only organization capable of handling such a sophisticated symposium.

With this said, I feel quite certain that when we reach the year 2000, we will be able to see the following fruits of our planning of the eighties which will certainly have elevated our professional status to the heights for which we dreamed.

This futuristic symposium should have a (proposed) agenda that covers the following:

First Day -	Geopolitical Environment, Threats, Accessment, Trends and issues.
Second Day -	Legal Trends and the Future
-	Social and Economical changes
-	Military Environment in which security would oper-

Third Day -

ate in the year 2000 and beyond.

Review of Security Applications covering a full spectrum of disciplines.

- Review of various standards and subcommittees recommendations for change.
- Technology topics.

This program should be focused to top level executives and security practitioners, researchers, academics and government officials.

Additional Security Advancements:

An International Academy of Security

This academy will be the focal point of all academic research, studies, planning and interdisciplinary coordination so badly needed to address ever-changing problems and issues. The Academy, of course, would be utilized in the every-day training efforts of professional development ranging from the security officer to the top executive.

Advanced Refinements in the Certified Protection Professional (CPP) Program Sponsored by ASIS

In the year 2000 there will still be a CPP Program, but, many changes in the requirements and operations will have been made. No one will be allowed to take the CPP Examination without at least a Bachelor's Degree. The CPP Examination will be multi-lingual in composition and will be internationally recognized as the basis for executive promotion and selection by private industry.

Expanded and Revised Security Academic Degree Programs

Practically every major college and university will be offering Baccalaureate and Masters Degree programs in Security Administration or related security programs. In view of the need, there will be greater emphasis placed on loss prevention, protection of assets and security management than on the now traditional Criminal Justice courses.

Eventually colleges will realize that the Security curriculum more properly belongs within the business division where proper emphasis can be placed on management concepts, as well as interrelationship with computer sciences and data processing courses.

Likewise, greater emphasis will be placed on behavioral sciences, high technology and forensic science applications to the protection of assets.

Professional School Recognition of Security's Increased Importance

There will be a tremendous increase in litigation which will necessitate introduction of specialized legal courses in our law schools, particularly relating to negligence, damage, and the protection of proprietary information as we move further into matters involving high technology.

Security courses will also be mandatory in other professional schools such as architecture, engineering and finance.

Inroads Into Public Law Enforcement

As our security line personnel become more professional in training, the demarcation lines now existing between public law enforcement and private security will gradually disappear. Many functions of Law Enforcement will be contracted out to private security.

Vulnerability Of High Technology To Sabotage, Espionage & Terrorism Will Require Heavy Security Presence

Although educational institutions today have not yet realized the need to incorporate security-type courses such as computer security and security management in their business curricula, these related courses will eventually become core courses.

Top level managers of firms must be cognizant of the change in from a manufacturing to an information economy.

Envoronmental Factors Will Require Active Security Participation

The complexities involved in environmental planning will require a diversified educational background on the part of security managers in order to adequately protect their firm's interests.

Included in such environmental planning will be site selection, VIP protection and a multitude of safety and security factors which make up risk management and emergency plannning. In addition, the threats of terrorism, industrial espionage, computer crime and a wide range of internal theft hazards will require our security personnel to be sufficiently equipped intellectually to develop adequate countermeasure responses.

Security Directors Will Occupy Top Level Management Positions

Our security managers in the year 2000 will no longer occupy an inferior position in the organizational structure of the firm. In fact, the Director of Security will function as an equal in top level management decision making processes and will be compensated accordingly.

This will be the true test of the professional progress of the private security practitioner. The title of CPP will earn the same respect as that of a CPA, and in most instances, the educational background could well exceed that of other business executives who are policy makers.

In conclusion, these are high hopes and the road to their realization will certainly be difficult. However, they are realistic and attainable. The substantial progress already made in such a short time by the pioneers of the private security profession is our best assurance for meeting these goals of the future.

Our greatest asset to our profession will be men and women who will dedicate themselves to be stewards of this noble undertaking to continue progress in our professional development as expeditiously as possible, but with a firm commitment to a code of ethics which espouses those essential moral precepts of truthfulness, honesty and integrity.

1. *Webster's New Collegiate Dictionary,* G. & C., Merriam Company, Springfield MA 1973, p. 919
2. *Private Security-Standards and Goals,* from the Official Private Security Task Force Report, by Arthur J. Bilek in 1977.

4

Moral & Social Implication in the Year 2000

Peter Hamilton, MBE, FRSA, FIPI, FINSTD

"An honest man, sir is able to speak for himself, when a knave is not."

SHAKESPEARE

Crime and Security in 2000

Not all the worst fears of George Orwell are likely to be realized this year. Nevertheless the intrusions into privacy which are now possible through electronic means do come somewhere near to his concept of the Thought Police.

If we could see into the future we might not like what we observe. I am reminded of a story by John Buchan called "The Gap in the Curtain." In this a number of distinguished men meet in a country house to listen to the prophesies of a mystic who undertook to show them a copy of *The Times* of one year hence. Two of them read their own obituary notice and the ensuing year was hardly a pleasant one for them.

It is, of course, the job of the intelligence specialist (that is my background) to discover that which is not known, and indeed to some extent to forecast future actions. The great Duke of Wellington said, "Most of the business of life is guessing what is at the other side of the hill."

So it is a very important matter to make reasonable judgements about the future so that we can prepare for it, but even if the security or intelligence man does make a good judgement about the future, he still has to convince the managers that security should be put in before the event, not afterwards. As most of us know, this is a very difficult matter.

It is true that I have in the past been fortunate enough to make some reasonably accurate prophesies. These may, of course, be intuitive, or sheer luck. I like to think that they have been reasonable inferences from discernable trends.

Some Examples of Prophesy

These are, I fear, personal and I adduce them only to show the process that I used and have used in the prophesies I shall make later on.

Some forty or more years ago I was in China, and at one stage it was my job to hold a press conference. One of the correspondents present wrote about this conference many years later when reviewing a book of mine. The press conference was conducted at a time when Chiang Kai-shek's last bastion was being systematically reduced to rubble by Japanese bombers . . . when the Imperial Japanese Navy was still a mighty force . . . when no one outside a handful of people . . . knew the atomic bomb was being developed. Hamilton said, "We will all be out of here in nine months," and he was politely laughed at. Less than a year later the Allied victory fleet steamed into Tokyo Bay.

I did not, of course, know about the atom bomb, but it seemed to be that there was a tremendous turning point in the morale of the Allies, and this is, as we know, the single most important factor in winning a war.

I also have made a few prophesies which, unfortunately, have been realized. For example, a problem with which we are currently concerned, computer security and the advent of the female terrorist, of whom more are anon. To me the first was a logical consequence of so powerful a development, the second of women's liberation.

I hope that these examples justify the following excursion into the future:

The Social Scene

I speak of this in relation only to the general setting for the crime and security scenarios that I am about to forecast. One does not need to be a sociologist to discern a gradual, and perhaps an increasingly less gradual, egalitarian trend - I speak of the Western democracies. This was certainly gradual until fairly recently because it was based to a large extent on the increased spread of education. It was natural that the more deprived sections of society should become more aware of what was on the rich man's table and should want to share in it - perfectly natural social evolution and, because of its gradualness, stable. But technology and the adman have so highly stimulated the appetites of many sections of society, if not all, that their desires in many cases cannot be satisfied. Any level of contentment which might have been possible in a gradually-changing society tends now to be destroyed by the continual pressure put upon them through the media to be discontented with their lot, so as to sell more of the ever-increasing range of consumer products.

The urge to keep up with the Joneses in the material sense has been accompanied by a changing view of what is right and what is wrong. The use of the office telephone for private calls, a general acceptance of cheap goods which have "fallen off a lorry," an increasing determination to be as exacting of the tax man is becoming of the taxpayer, together with many other features, suggest a sharply declining property morality. Thus is the distinction between right and wrong, lawful and unlawful, being blurred.

This is the seedbed in which most nastier forms of crime can grow and flourish. In one sense, the major criminals have a better chance of not being detected, since a large part of the population is itself, engaged in some form of less serious crime, and at the same time the successful petty criminal of today becomes the successful major criminal of the future.

I see no chance of reversing these trends in the next decade, if ever.

So my first prophesy is that there will be more and more people engaged in, and sympathetic to crime than ever before.

We must now examine what will grow in this criminal climate.

The Direction of Crime

There is little doubt in my mind that violence and fraud will be the leaders. The present threshold of violence in our society is very low. Many people seem ready to turn to violence on the slightest pretext, and this is particularly true of young people. We increasingly hear of the beating up of schoolteachers and elderly people by teenagers.

A London taxi-driver told me a story which well illustrates this point. He normally went on duty at six o'clock in the morning, but on one day decided to go in late. He saw that his two sons starting out for school were carrying knuckledusters. He asked them why and was informed that it was "beat-up-teacher" day, and that this was a regular occurrence. The father asked why they were not punished. They told him that the teacher had been informed that if she reported them, things would be far worse for her and she would be really seriously beaten up. The taxi-driver protested strongly and the older of the boys said, "Better be careful Dad, or we'll have to bring the gang round to see you."

We all know the sad trends in violence associated with competitive games, especially soccer.

It is not easy to explain the dramatic rise in violence of all forms, but I advance the following two reasons:

The first is the natural violence in us has normally had a regular outlet through war which now, mainly because of nuclear weapons, no longer provides such an outlet.

Secondly, because of modern technology and the welfare state, we no longer have to struggle to survive. In fact, we can sit all day, do nothing, and still survive.

None of the factors which I suggest underlie the rise in violence is likely to change, and hence I see its continued growth.

70

Fraud is the other obvious growth area. Here I see both major fraud and mass but minor fraud increasing. Major fraud is likely to be rewarding for two main reasons: One is that modern technology and industrial and commercial progress permit the concentration of enormous amounts of money. Secondly, there are and will continue to be, long periods of time before fraud is discovered. A very great deal of fraud is discovered when the fraudsters get too greedy and obviously change their lifestyles. Minor fraud by the masses is unlikely to change. The use of the office telephone for private calls is unlikely to change. The use of the office telephone for private calls is unlikely to diminish, and it has to be remembered that the telephone theft gives rise to two other thefts: the company's time and the tax on the benefit. This is a large chunk of the so-called black economy. No doubt to this may be added pens, pencils and paper.

An additional reason why fraud will continue to grow is the increasing number of person technically able to defeat accounting procedures, especially when they are of an electronic nature.

As we know, there is an enormous home video industry. When this is syndicated, as it is by various criminal gangs, it becomes exceptionally damaging to the video companies, and even the home video industry is not without impact.

Counterfeiting, a form of fraud, is not confined to Taiwan. Like the pirating referred to above, it is an extensive and threatening industry. Pharmaceutical drugs have been counterfeited with consequent danger to life, and brand names in the drink trade have been counterfeited, again with danger to those who consume the products. This is another crime which becomes easier with modern technology to imitate labels and packaging.

No doubt other types of fraud will arise as society develops, and indeed each development, such as the computer, creates new criminal possibilities. But perhaps the most serious aspect of crime of the future will be its pervasiveness. So many people will be engaged in it in low or high degree that it will come to be tolerated and will be the more difficult to defeat because our policemen and security men are, of course, drawn from that very society.

The Political Criminal

Two German nineteenth-century military philosophers (they were also men of action) prophesied in different ways that the absence of war, to which I have already referred, might create more problems than war itself. Neither of them, of course, was aware of the development of nuclear weapons. The first of these and perhaps the less philosophical, was General Bernhardi, who said quite simply, "War is a biological necessity." The second, and perhaps one of the finest soldiers of all time, was Field Marshal Conrad von Moltke. When in his old age a friend suggested that eternal peace was a desirable end, von Moltke, horror-struck, replied, "In that case, it will be replaced by materialism."

If von Moltke was wrong in not desiring peace, there is very little doubt that he was totally right about materialism, which is the creeping crisis of our age, manifest in almost all sections of Western society. It is arguable that materialism or greed is the biggest single cause of the Western crime wave. The job of the security man, however, is to deal with the crime phenomenon as best he can. He cannot be expected to deal with cause. He must stick to dealing with effect.

Until the last couple of decades, the security profession's acquaintance with political crime was limited to the provision of equipment. Today a vast and growing part of that profession is concerned with giving advice and assistance to the potential victims of political dissidents who will not hesitate to use violence in pursuit of their aims. These terrorists today are mostly of what is commonly called the left wing. Their methods and philosophies are almost identical with those of the extreme right from which Europe, in particular, has suffered severely this century.

Political crime takes a number of forms:
1. Terrorism, i.e., direct violence.
2. Brainwashing - particularly by false prophets of the East, usually based on the United States with the prophet

prophet owning many Rolls-Royces.

3. Actions and inactions which, while non-violent in themselves, are designed to provoke violence from the forces of law and order. In this way the organizers of such events can attribute the violence which they themselves have caused to those whom they wish to destroy.

No one needs to be given examples of category 1 - terrorism, or category 2 - brainwashing, since these are really too well known, but the third calls for some explanation.

There are two main sub-categories. The first is action by organized labor to deprive society of its essential services such as water, electricity and so on. This has been comparatively commonplace in the last decade in the United Kingdom and has been successful in bringing down a government, and is thus political. The second comprises actions such as the ladies of Greenham Common, some of whom are, of course, genuinely concerned, but a large number of whom are concerned to defeat the basis of our political system - the ballot-box.

French farmers who peacefully sabotage the freedom of trade to which their government subscribes provoke violence for their own political ends, which are undoubtedly designed to make the Common Agricultural Policy work only in favor or France.

My prophesy: Within fifteen years' time the ability of the police to deal with the political criminal - and I include the ladies of Greenham Common and the French farmers in this term - will be limited by the sheer weight of the problem, and the security man who is responsive to commercial considerations will take over much of their role.

I have deliberately left a fourth category of political criminals to the last part of this section because I consider them to be in many ways the most dangerous of all. These are those who are prepared to use criminal means of violence to deprive the great majority of their legitimate interests and activities, including their sporting activities. In Britain, particularly, there are organized groups, usually with a Marxist background, who under the guise of animal welfare, for which most of them care not at all, are prepared to attack physically and morally the lawful right of others to hunt vermin, to shoot pheasants and to fish. They increasingly deny the right of people to eat animals. They don't choose to try to impose their views via the ballot box because they know they could never win by that route.

One is tempted to speculate that if they succeeded in depriving the majority of the right to eat meat, their next ploy would be to sympathize with the feelings of the soya bean which forms the basis for the plastic steak. If they did so, it would be entirely for political reasons.

Ludicrous though it may seem, the security man will be involved in protecting the rights of the majority, who undoubtedly will continue to wish to be carnivorous. Already security men are being hired by masters of foxhounds, and it seems likely that fishing streams, ponds and lakes will have to have access control against angling saboteurs.

Security in the Year 2000

I would expect security in the Western democracies to be one of the biggest industries, with the numbers employed correspondingly high. In Great Britain alone, I would expect there to be more than a million men directly employed in the security industry, or in closely related manufacturing industries. I will give an estimated breakdown of this figure but first I want to try to answer the obvious question: What will be the size and role of the police forces in the democracies?

Allowing for the differences in the structure of the various police forces of the West, I would estimate that there will be little numerical change. For example, in Great Britain our police forces total over one hundred thousand. Any substantial enlargement would be politically and perhaps financially impossible, but I would expect to see a big change in their role.

In the first place, they will all be armed, including the British ones. Because of increased violence, I expect them to have much more fire power than can be provided by side arms. Rubber bullets, water cannon, weapons capable of delivering gas canisters, and automatic weapons will be held in every major police station. They will also have armored cars.

In a word, the majority of police will become quasi-military with military-type communications which many of them have already, an increased ability to concentrate large numbers at short notice, and their own bomb disposal facilities. There will be specially designed mobile obstacles for efficient crowd control. One of these already in existence is a tractor-type vehicle capable of laying a triple-dannaert barbed wire fence a hundred meters long in a few minutes.

As a result of this quasi-military role, the ability of the police to deal with crime other than armed violence will be seriously diminished. In a rising tide of robbery, burglary, fraud, including credit card fraud, unbridled violence against individuals - women, the elderly and weak - with the police unable to cope, there will be massive demands for security.

Categories needing protection

Some of the categories of persons and property which will need a high degree of protection are the following:
VIPs
Diplomatic Missions
Nurses
Schoolteachers
The elderly
Public idols
Non-unionized small businesses and their proprietors
Shoppers at Christmas time
Those with sufficient knowledge to create nuclear weapons under duress
Judges, jurors and lawyers
Public utility key points, e.g., power stations, electricity distribution networks, including transformers and switching stations, reservoirs and water pumping stations, sewage systems, communications and telecommunications
Hospitals, particularly their drug stores
Pharmacists and associated stocks in warehouses
Jewelry shops
Precious stone bourses
Banks

Validation centres of credit card companies
Computers
. . . and so on

The Role and Shape of the Security Industry in 2000

The security industry will consist of the following elements:
Advisory and Planning - Systems will be tailor-made for the job experts, sometimes in-house and sometimes external consultants. Almost certainly consultants will be called in from time-to-time to advise on updating. Security consultancy service may be independent, or may be grafted onto firms of architects or engineers. These services will replace those currently offered by manufacturers whose main interest is in purveying their own goals.

The security manufacturers working to obligatory standards. Security computers will form a large part of this industry.

Corporate security officers. It will be a condition of insurance coverage that a properly qualified corporate security man be a member of the management of every medium and large firm.

Guards - static and mobile. These by law will have to be highly trained and well-versed in electronic extensions of their senses. They may well be armed. As there will not be sufficient police manpower to answer alarm calls, this will be carried out by special squads of security men based in commercial central alarm stations. These will be capable of dealing with armed robbers, hijackers and the like.

Investigation. This service will be a far cry from the former private eye employed in divorce cases. This service will consist of persons *highly trained* in investigative and detective skills. Criminal records will be, by law, available to them. They will have three main functions: first, of inquiring into the backgrounds of applicants for sensitive appointments in industry and commerce; secondly, of after care surveillance of persons in sensitive appointments; thirdly, of investigating successful crimes other than those investigated by the police.

Research and Development. Facilities will be set up in selected universities to research and improve methods, equipment, and standards within the security profession.

Insurance. Insurance will become an acknowledged part of the wider discipline of security. Property and perhaps personal insurance will only be obtainable on the certificate of a qualified security man to the effect that the proposer has taken all reasonable security steps in light of the threat.

From the above emerges the likely role of security in 2000. It will be a recognized profession subject to government license and thus accountable to a greater extent than the security man of today, who now is no more accountable than any other citizen. It may be argued that the result will be merely the creation of another police force. This is not so. There will be the following major differences:

1. The individual person or company will have to pay directly for their security. The amount, at a guess, will be between ten and twenty percent of a person's income. There will be security aid for those who cannot afford proper precautions.

2. Because of the nature of the security industry, a large part of it being within the organization, the security man will be within the private area of industry and commerce and thus in a far better position to deal with the criminal problem there than the police, who only have access to the private area in special circumstances - usually after the crime has been committed.

Some Novelties

No doubt there will be much technological development, both in crime and security. It is impossible to foresee all of this, but I believe the most interesting will be in the field of investigative computers and of interception of telecommunications.

It is well known that quite simple computers can materially assist doctors in diagnosis by a programmed question and answer technique. While these do not necessarily have a better diagnostic capability than the best doctors and scientists, they can have universal application. It has been discovered in trials that patients afraid to tell the doctor everything are much more inclined to tell the whole truth to a computers.

It would seem that similar techniques could be employed in the selection of persons for key appointments. It also has to be said that no doubt such computers could be used for interrogation of suspects. Society may, of course, ban such methods, but this will not stop criminals from using computers for their own purposes.

Since information is the lifeblood of almost all our activities, and increasingly so, it is to be expected that there will be a big increase in the bugging of all forms of telecommunication, whether landline, radio or satellite. This will lead to various forms of enciphering, and in turn the cryptanalyst will have an important role to play. Electronic money will almost certainly be attacked.

The punk rock band that made a hoax recording of a top secret conversation between Prime Minister Thatcher and President Reagan have demonstrated a new horror. This anarchist group put together a tape from parts of TV and radio broadcasts and attempted to deliver it to newspapers across the world, timed to arrive shortly before the British general election in 1983. It might be possible to trigger off a nuclear war by this means.

Conclusion

There can be little doubt in one's mind that by 2000 we shall, if we do not take adequate precautions, be living in a criminal climate of a greater size and danger than ever before. The powerful security industry predicted will without doubt reduce the liberty of the individual, but less so than will rampant crime.

Society must make its choice.

5

Security Management of the Future

Oliver O. Wainwright, CPP

Security is the most exciting profession in industry today. The practitioner is required to focus on the entire spectrum of corporate activity as well as on the environment in which corporations operate. While both conflict and opportunity can be found in the security field, it is safe to say there is more opportunity than conflict. Security professionals must not only capitalize on the opportunities of today, but also identify, understand, and manage the opportunities that will arise in the future.

Studying the future is crucial for the astute security professional.[1] Critics of the field often mention the inability of practitioners to relate research and program efforts to the strategic or future perspectives of business. Futures methodology — the use of analytical methods to study and influence the future — can be used to counter this criticism.

Security has been defined as the use of "measures designed to safeguard personnel, to prevent unauthorized access to equipment, facilities, materials, and documents, and to safeguard them against espionage, sabotage, theft, and fraud."[2] This definition has withstood the test of time and probably will not change significantly in the future. What is changing, however, is the organizational environment in which these words apply.

The transition from smokestack industries to an information economy will require security practitioners to relate to a new kind of organization in the future. The information age, With its associated technologies, is causing the creation of more decentralized organizations with integrated networks.[3] As a result, the security practitioner will need to understand the formal and informal movement of security programs through complex organizations. Training in the intuitive management and a global view of the organization's environment will be necessary.[4] Security practitioners will need to establish the link between the security function and various business and environmental issues that affect the organization.

Most security practitioners use some method to evaluate the likelihood that certain events will occur, generally some form of probability theory — subjective, objective, or conditional.[5] But this approach falls short for both investigations and program management of the future because it concentrates on discrete events rather than on a rigorous analysis of trends and changes over time. This failing is understandable since we live in a society geared to short-term outcomes.[6] But the rapid growth of technology we now face requires looking farther ahead and visualizing consequences.

This change in focus is needed particularly in the security field where, traditionally, practitioners have not analyzed their environment as systematically or as rigorously as their counterparts in marketing, finance, and other corporate functions. As a result, many organizations of great accomplishment face high risk because they are not protected adequately from the wave of change generated by technology. Security practitioners often overlook a programmed approach to security research and a strategy for integrating research findings into corporate decision making.

One approach for resolving this organizational management. Appropriately named futuristics,[7] studies of this kind enable the security practitioner to put security management of the future into the proper perspective. Note that the focus is not on security management *in* the future, but rather security management *of* the future.

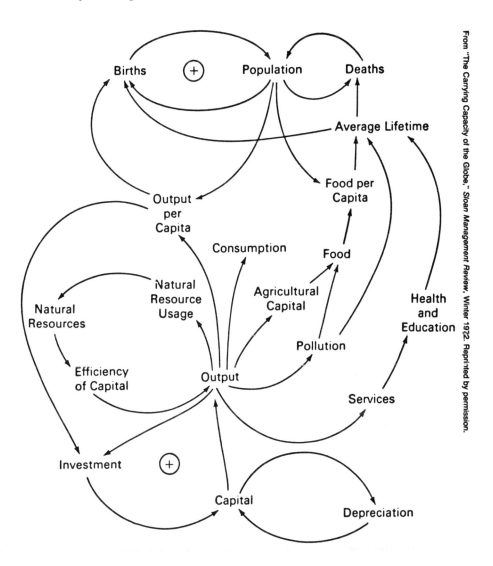

From "The Carrying Capacity of the Globe," *Sloan Management Review,* Winter 1972. Reprinted by permission.

Exhibit 1
A Causal Model Showing Patterns of Environmental
Influence for a Manufacturing Firm

Several analytical and forecasting techniques in the futuristics field are a natural fit for the security practitioner concerned about security management of the future. One technique applies causal models, which are based on the assumption that all of the factors influencing change in a given situation are known. The cause/effect relationships in the model should be depicted in a way that reduces complexity, simplifies understanding, and aids in visualizing the shape of the future events and trends.

Exhibit 1 is a universal causal model that shows patterns of environmental influence for manufacturing firms.[8] The model shows that output affects various business, environmental, and life cycles. While the model does not give precise information on the cause/effect relationships represented by each arrow, it does depict patterns of influence. Organizations outside of manufacturing can adapt this model to their situation by substituting variables based on their own strategic planning and mapping different sets of cause/effect relationships.

By studying the model in Exhibit 1, some interesting conclusions can be drawn. A positive relationship exists between capital and investments and output. However, it is clear that output also generates pollution, which affects agricultural capital, food, food per capita, and ultimately the average lifetime of the population.

A security director of a manufacturing firm with patterns of influence similar to those in Exhibit 1 should become attuned to pollution issues, which are being scrutinized by governments and special interest groups now and will continue to be watched in the future. The firm's actions under the legal doctrine of reasonable care will require security involvement in environmental planning. Verification of waste disposal processes will also need to be monitored directly or through liaison with law enforcement.

Another analytical technique used by futurists is the Delphi process.[9] In this process, a chairman or consensus builder devises a question or issue statement and solicits several rounds of responses from selected specialists and experts who offer their opinions independently. Through the compilation and analysis of their responses, a consensus view on the issue can be formed, yet differing viewpoints can be considered.

The Delphi process is particularly appropriate to security management of the future. Let's assume, for example, that the corporate director of security for a major high technology corporation has been asked by top management to determine the years during which the corporation will be most vulnerable to espionage and sabotage. To formulate an answer through the Delphi process, several members of the corporate management team are asked to participate, including knowledgeable sources from corporate planning, human resources, finance, marketing, R&D, distribution, and manufacturing, as well as security. Input from many corporate sources works well in this case because the answer is critical not only to security but also to the company's overall strategic business plan.

In round one of the Delphi process, the question "In what years will this corporation be most vulnerable to espionage and sabotage?" is distributed to the participants. They respond and give an indepth explanation of their views based on the long-range planning in their specialty and the overall corporate strategic plans.

Numerical answers typical of those that might be given by the management respondents have been arranged chronologically in **Exhibit 2.** The year 1995 emerges as the mean, or average, of the responses. The middle 50 percent of the responses, the inner quartile, falls between 1988 and 2002.

Exhibit 2
Delphi Computation Showing the Inner Quartile Range

1985	1987	1989	1991	1993	1995	1997	1999	2001	2003	2004

Mean

Inner Quartile (middle 50 percent)
of the Responses

In round two of the Delphi process, the director of security distributes the information in Exhibit 2 to the participants. Respondents whose answers were outside the inner quartile are asked why their judgment differs from the majority view, causing those with extreme views to explain their positions or revise them to fall within the inner quartile range.

During the next round, participants receive the revised findings and can again modify their responses. Round four repeats the procedure, giving respondents a final chance to reconsider before the final inner quartile range is identified.

For additional futures research, the security director may choose to focus on the median year of the responses or might develop a series of scenarios for each of the years in the inner quartile. The reasons given by the respondents for why corporate vulnerability to espionage and sabotage might peak in each of the years in the range could lead to plans of alternatives for corporate security efforts in the future.

The Delphi process does have its drawbacks. The first, of course is the long time required to reach a final opinion. Second, the leader must have strong support from top management so the question, responses, and analysis are appropriate. Since the data generated will only be as good as the expertise of the participants, management must be willing to devote time to the project.[10] Still, the pitfalls of "groupthink" are avoided because the participants are kept separate.[11] Respondents feel no pressure to conform, encouraging openness, dissent, and a clear appraisal of the issues.

Security Program Components	Protecting Proprietary Information	Security of Computers/Telecommunication	Security of R&D/Marketing Information	Guard Operations	Investigations	Crisis Management	Executive Protection	Security Training/Awareness	Employee Relations	Substance Abuse Programs	Security of Product Distribution	Raw Score	Normalized Score
Protecting Proprietary Information	✕	8	8	4	8	8	4	8	2	2	4	56	11.8%
Security of Computers/Telecommunications	8	✕	8	1	4	8	1	8	1	1	2	42	8.8
Security of R&D/Marketing Information	3	8	✕	4	3	8	2	4	1	2	4	49	10.3
Guard Operations	4	2	4	✕	2	8	4	2	4	4	4	38	8.0
Investigations	8	4	8	4	✕	8	8	2	1	4	8	55	11.6
Crisis Management	8	8	4	4	2	✕	8	4	2	1	4	45	9.5
Executive Protection	4	2	2	2	4	8	✕	8	2	1	1	34	7.2
Security Training/Awareness	8	8	8	4	2	8	4	✕	4	4	2	52	10.9
Employee Relations	8	8	4	4	2	4	1	4	✕	2	4	41	8.6
Substance Abuse Programs	4	2	4	2	4	1	1	4	4	✕	2	28	5.9
Security of Product Distribution	2	4	2	4	8	8	1	4	1	1	✕	35	7.4
												475	100%

Exhibit 3—Cross Support Matrix

Raw Score   Normalized Score

In view of the espionage and sabotage problems expected to occur in the years cited by the Delphi participants, the security director of this high technology firm should continue futuristic research. Cross-support matrix analysis is an appropriate technique at this point, because it allows the security director to examine how existing security program components might be affected by espionage and sabotage in each of the critical years identified in the Delphi process.

Exhibit 3 is an example of a cross-support matrix that might be developed for the median year, 1995. The security program components, listed at the top and side of the matrix, are identified by the security director. The matrix is distributed to the members of the management team who participated in the Delphi process.

Each expert fills in the cells across the rows based on his or her opinion of what security components will be most crucial in 1995 to protect the company adequately against the high vulnerability to espionage and sabotage expected in that year. In Exhibit 3, the following numberical scale is used for the responses:[12]

— very high
— moderate
— low
— negligible

In selecting a response, each participant considers how the need to implement each security component at the left of the matrix in 1995 affects the security of computers/telecommunications, the security of R&D/marketing information, guard operations, investigations, and so on across the columns of the matrix. The numeral assigned to each cell is supported by a detailed explanation from each expert. Once the matrix has been completed, the responses are returned to the security director, who computes the normalized score using the following equation: 1 / *sum of raw scores* X *raw score-normalized score*. The normalized score represent percentages or weights for each program component, which can then be used for comparison and planning purposes.

To explain further, let's assume the results of the Delphi process show the company will be especially vulnerable to sabotage and espionage in 1995 because a revolutionary new product line will be introduced in that year. Exhibit 3, a hypothetical example, shows the respondent feels the ability of the company to secure proprietary information eleven years hence will have a very high (8) effect on the security of computers/telecommunications, the security of R&D/marketing information, investigations, crisis management, and security training/awareness. It will have a moderate (4) effect on guard operation, executive protection, and the security of product distribution, but only a minimal (2) effect on employee relations and substance abuse programs.

After computing the normalized scores, the security director is able to see which security components should receive the greatest emphasis by 1995 to protect the corporation adequately from espionage and sabotage. In our example, the greatest efforts should be directed toward protecting proprietary information (including R&D/marketing data), investigations, and security training/awareness.

The information in this matrix can also provide the basis for scenario building, a popular futures research method because corporate decision makers can apply their judgments to various conditions expected in the future. Common threads may emerge from basic scenarios submitted by the experts, which the security director can translate into a surprise-free scenario, one that has a high probability of occurring because it includes common events pulled from all the scenarios.[13]

Scenario building has many advantages in that it draws from historical events as well as plausible and likely implications that might be overlooked in conventional planning. The technique should not be confused with security planning. It can, however, be used as a lead into effective planning methods.

Backward planning, as an extension of scenario building, is another futures research technique suited to security. [14] The security director initiates the process by devising a conceptual view of security at some future time, for instance 1995, the year the high technology firm in our examples is expected to be most vulnerable to sabotage and espionage. In backward planning, the members of the management team who have participated in the other futures research techniques are asked to identify changes in security programs that should take place each year to reach appropriate levels of security in 1995.

Exhibit 4: Backward Planning Chart

1995 *Double the investigative staff/code all documents electronically/provide 20 hrs of sec. training to all empl*
1993 *hire add'l investigators/encode documents/provide monthly sec. training*
1991 *hire add'l investigators/purchase document encoding equipment*
1989 *hire add'l investigators/provide bi-monthly security training*
1987 *hire add'l investigators/concentrate on sec. training for R&D/market'g*
1985 *hire add'l investigators/provide quarterly security training*

Exhibit 4 is an example of a backward planning chart. The factors listed for each year could be analyzed further through causal models, cross-support matrix analysis, scenario building, or additional backward planning.

Effective security management of the future can still fit the time-tested definition mentioned at the beginning of this article. However, the challenge is clear: we must measure the impact of technology and develop our own alternative security futures. Futuristics methodology is a good way to approach the complexity caused by technological and social change.

About the Author . . . *Oliver O. Wainwright, CPP, is corporate manager of security for SCM Corporation, New York, NY. He is a certified security trainer and board member of the Academy of Security Educators and Trainers. A member of ASIS, Wainwright serves on the Society's Standing Committee on Physical Security. He is also a member of the World Future Society.*

1. Robert M. Fulmer, "Profiles of the Future — The Management Tomorrow," *Business Horizons* (August 1972), p. 5.
2. US Army, *FM 1930 Physical Security* (March 1979), pp. 1-7, 298-293.
3. William E. Halal, "Organization of the Future," Defense Intelligence Futuristics and Creative Analysis seminar (Washington, DC, 1978).
4. Weston H. Agor, "Tomorrow's Intuitive Leaders," *The Futurist* (August 1983), pp. 49-53.
5. Jack A. Kinney, "Analytical Investigative Methods," course in Advanced Techniques for Investigators, Virginia State Police Academy (Richmond, VA, 1983).

6. John Naisbitt, *Megatrends: Ten New Directions Transforming our Lives* (New York: Warner Books, Inc., 1982), pp. 79-96.
7. Draper L. Kauffman, Jr., *Futurism and Futures Studies* (Washington, DC: National Education Association, 1976), p. 11.
8. Ibid.
9. Joseph F. Coates, "Planning for a New Industrial Revolution, Techniques and Tools," World Future Society workshop (Washington, DC, 1983).
10. Marvin Centron, "Technological Forecasting Techniques," Defense Intelligence seminar (Washington, DC, 1983).
11. Irving L. Janis, *Victims of Groupthink* (Boston: Houghton Mifflin Company, 1967), pp. 1-6.
12. Ibid.
13. Coates, "Planning for a New Industrial Revolution."
14. "Planning Techniques," Center for Future Management workshop (Washington, DC, 1978).

6

Safeguarding Proprietary Information — 2000

Brian R. Hollstein, CPP

Manager, Corporate Security, Xerox Corporation, Stamford,
James A. Schweitzer, System Security Technology Manager,
Xerox Corporation, Stamford, CT

"Without an appreciation of the larger shifts that are restructuring our society, we act on assumptions that are out of date. Out of touch with the present, we are doomed to fail in the unfolding future."

JOHN NAISBITT, *MEGATRENDS*

One of more influential books written so far this decade is *Megatrends* by John Naisbitt. In it, he projects the future from ten trends clearly visible today. Three trends which he identifies are of considerable interest to us because they will have a strong Impact on the way proprietary information will be protected and managed in the future:

- industrial — information
- centralization — decentralization
- hierarchies — networking.

With all due respect to Mr. Naisbitt's brilliant work, we will try to briefly summarize each of these trends and examine them in the light of our need for protection of proprietary information.

Industrial — information

In the latter part of this century we are witnessing the process of conversion of the U.S. economy from one based on the production of goods to an economy based on the production, dissemination and use of information. Our smoke stack industries are finding it increasingly difficult to compete with the new capital equipment and cheap labor overseas.

The U.S. has been the originator and chief benefactor of the electronic revolution due to our innovations in computing and communications equipment. Although we are importing a larger and larger percentage of our manufactured goods, the world economy is more and more dependent on the U.S.' unparalleled system of satellites, terrestrial communications, computers and software. Without these information systems, the ability to make and distribute goods would be severely hampered. Mr. Naisbitt notes a very significant trend - in 1940, 17% of American workers were involved in information management. In the early part of this decade, approximately 65% of the American workers are involved in information management jobs[1]. It is interesting to note that between 1875 and 1975 not much had changed in the typical office. All the essentials for operation of the business office were designed for handling pieces of paper. Business thinking contains words intended for the paper oriented communication systems. Words like memo, letter, message and file all mean pieces of paper. In box, out box, reference files, calendar, telephone message note, file cabinet, notebook, folder are all means of managing paper. Two significant changes have occurred though in the process of dealing with business communications. The first was the telephone about 100 years ago, and although there have been many improvements in the telephone, it is still used in the original way — that is a hand held instrument used for conversation between two individuals. Highly sophisticated advance products which are often advertised have not yet come into general use. The integrity of proprietary information has long been threatened by the wire tap. Society has come to grips with this problem through legislation, law enforcement and education.

The second major change in the office was the introduction of the plain paper copier which eliminated much of the need for carbons, stencils, etc., and allowed transmission of paper-based information in parallel. That is a memo writer could now send a memo to 20 people and assume they would all get the message at about the same time as compared to serial delivery of an original via the old "routing slip." The copy machine has become a prime tool for information "leaks" to the press, competitors and foreign governments.

Since 1975, the office workplace is being revolutionized through the use of electronics. This revolution is gaining speed rapidly and we can expect that within the next 20 years most offices will be heavily automated. Information systems and office automation are two examples of technology developments which are changing the way businesses handle information. They directly concern the managers charged with the security of business information. The changes are coming ever more rapidly as the result of key developments in computing technology which allow an increasing scale of circuit integration using silicon crystals. Hundreds of thousands of tiny circuits can be placed and interconnected on Very Large Scale Integrated (VLSI) chips one tenth the size of a postage stamp. Past experience has shown that the number of components per chip has doubled every year since 1960 and there is no indication that this trend will stop in the near future.

There are three main results of research and engineering of computers apparent to us today:

- Computing power is extremely cheap in comparison to the relative inflation of other goods and services In the past 25-30 years. In fact, the cost of processing has decreased about 25% per year. Wages certainly haven't, so there are strong economic pressures to use computers.

- Computer hardware and software efficiency has improved remarkably. 800 million operations per second is currently possible and make large data base processing attractive. Distributed processing networks are also made possible through control data storage and rapid large file processes.

- Miniaturization of computer circuits has been made possible by advances in solid state technology. Computing power which was only available in large control processors a few years ago now sits in the corner of a desk.

Security thinking has remained behind the leading edge of technology application. A security "gap" developed during the 1960s and 1970s. Information security planners failed to grasp the importance of the development of computers in terms of safeguarding information. Security efforts remained largely physical in nature to protect hardware while information took on non-physical forms such as electronically generated digital or analog signals. While systems, finance, industrial engineering and other fields rapidly applied computing power to their disciplines, security has continued to regard the world as paper oriented.

Information in electronic forms has qualities which are novel and startling.

- Information is not limited by physical distances.
- Access to information does not require physical presence.
- Retrieval of information from electronic files can be invisible, even to the computer.
- A small disk or other memory media can store huge volumes of information.

The very existence of information technology encourages and enables people to work ever more efficiently on developing newer and better systems. Computing power is being made available at the personal level at work and at home in forms which are increasingly simple to use and extremely cheap to operate. There are many thinkers who predict that we will be moving into total automation in the workplace, the "paperless office." We do not feel that paper will be eliminated entirely from the office systems, however, it will be playing a decidedly minor part, mainly as emergency backup for electronic systems. The evolution, or perhaps revolution, of the personal workplace is being driven by competitive pressures for productivity improvements across the total workforce. Investments in the facilities provided to knowledge workers has been only 1/8 that of investment in factories, and as a result, factory productivity has increased markedly over the past 10 years while office productivity has remained static. With human labor costs escalating steeply and a growing majority of workers in the white collar and service industries, startling improvements in the cost/benefits equation for electronics makes microcomputing a key opportunity for providing value-added efficiencies to knowledge of workers. In some cases, electronics will supplant or displace human labor in the office, thus offering tremendous leverage for productivity gains. Another effect of the increased use of computers in the workplace has been that we are finding that our products have a much shorter life cycle. In the past, a basic product might have a life span of 25 or 30 years. Over this time span, the product was slowly improved, but not radically changed. Modern products, especially "high tech," very often have a life cycle of only 2 or 3 years. This means that the enormous sums spent on research and development need to be recouped over a much shorter period of time. The competition to design and manufacture products with such short life cycles becomes fierce and many of the competitors turn to extra legal, or in some cases, illegal means to remain in the competition. All of this leads us to the conclusion that as time and technology advances continue, information will be an extremely important commodity which must be protected if the business structure is to grow and prosper.

Security of information in the electronic office will require cheap encryption, improved software, and operating systems which are user friendly, with security included. Many of the aspects of traditional security procedures for handling of paper can be replicated in the security systems of electronic data processing equipment. Physical security for large central processing units is well established and it does not present a serious challenge to the security professional. Good security software for the central processing unit is readily available today and is relatively cheap. Encryption during transmission of data provides a virtually foolproof method of protection of that information. However, as we follow the trend towards increasing decentralization of computing power, so that everyone has the ability to manipulate data at his workstation, we discover that these traditional systems break down almost immediately. While the security systems in large central processing units force, in may instances, compliance with security requirements, the decentralized process depends almost entirely on the individual user's awareness of security needs and willingness to comply with the rules. It is not unusual for very large networks of users to have easy access to each other's work in progress due to the tremendous popularity in networking systems. It can be anticipated that with the growth and increasing complexity of these networks, that information protection will become an extremely difficult tasks. Based on experience to date we can expect that encryption will become increasingly cheaper to install even in small units. Certainly software programs will be developed which will aid in protecting information on the office systems. However, the ability and willingness of the individual worker to ensure that security systems actually work and are used is a completely different matter. It is incumbent upon the security manager today to become aware of the complexities of the systems which are being installed and to be preparing a program which will enable him or her to develop the security needs along with the technology.

Centralization — decentralization

The next of Naisbitt's trends which we would like to examine is the centralization — decentralization phenomenon. Naisbitt makes the observation that there is a great political shift going on in the United States from a centralized federal government solving the problems of the American people to a more diversified local government solving the problems of its local constituents. This is coming about as centralized solutions fail to address local problems and needs. We see more political power going to specialized interest groups working on strictly local matters of local interest. If I may take the liberty of extending Naisbitt's arguments to the business world, we are witnessing similar trends. Big companies are finding that traditional hierarchical business structures are not able to effectively manage in an age of great and rapid change. A greater autonomy must be afforded individual managers of products meeting diverse markets and different competition. The computer, and more specifically distributed processing, backed by instant electronic communication, places access to information in a rapid and timely manner in the hands of all employees. While this greatly enhances the business process, security of information becomes a major challenge. With technology available today, a month's worth of correspondence can be stored on a 6" floppy disk. It takes two minutes to copy the disk or transmit the information to a distant location. We can anticipate that storage capacity of a disk will increase enormously over the next five years and that transmission time will drop. In the past, theft of information depended on obtaining access to paper files and use of a copier or camera to duplicate the information. All of this takes time and equipment and carries with it the possibility of discovery - besides, breaking and entering is illegal. Electronic theft of information using present technology can be swift and painless *for the thief.* As our systems of computer processing and communications become more complex, we can expect a tremendous increase in exposure to loss of information.

As Mr Naisbitt notes, traditional centralized organizations, whether they be business or government, are undergoing a process of change brought on by the breakdown of centralized institutions in the 1960's and 70's. Competition with the Japanese has led to an analysis of their clustered decentralized working groups. As more technology entered our society, people have become impatient with bureaucracy and are demanding more personal interaction and decision powers. And finally, a generation of young people came into the work place with work expectations which found traditional organizations "foreign, unnatural".

Hierarchies — networking

Many of us as security practitioners have felt these effects in our own organizations. Our security hierarchies and traditional discipline in which everyone knows the "proper way to act" have been placed to the test on more than one occasion. The return to a more conservative orientation during the first half of the eighties has not completely erased the changes already in evidence. Hierarchical structures are still in place, Naisbitt says, but many people no longer believe that they are the best way to proceed in business organization. Networking has evolved as an informal way to "grease the wheels" of a rusty hierarchical system and make it not more efficient, but to make it more human. Naisbitt describes networks as "exist(ing) to foster self help, to exchange information, to change society, to improve productivity and work life, and to share resources. They are structured to transmit information in a way that is quicker, more high tech, and more energy efficient than any other process we know."[2] The networking trend is important to us when it is coupled with computers, communications and proprietary information. Nowhere is networking more apparent than in the informal computer electronic bulletin boards which have sprung up by the hundreds all over the U.S. Everything from bread recipes to dating ads, technical discussions and programs, or used cars for sale, are posted on these electronic bulletin boards for easy access to all. It is not unusual to note on some computer hobbyists' bulletin boards instructions for obtaining information from credit card companies or telephone numbers of computing equipment which may be penetrated in order to obtain free services. In fact, with the advent of personal computing, the philosophy of its users has been oriented to free sharing of information and skills. This free sharing coupled with the tendency to want to evade regulation (except the iron bound discipline of programming) makes for difficulties for the security function which wants to limit the dissemination of proprietary data.

We also find that networking extends across company boundaries. Traditionally, computer people have been more loyal to their discipline that to their employer. Computer scientist and technicians tend to live in a separate world from the normal business activity. Businessmen could not and did not understand them with their arcane jargon and clannish ways. Because of its youth, the computing industry does not have a well established inner structure of codes of ethical behavior. Emphasis on the big money of an extremely fast moving industry in which young men can become millionaires virtually overnight, can make temptations to pirate ideas and technical information irresistible. Networking and breakdown of traditional loyalties to employers are excellent conduits to the loss of information. Another trend is the return to cottage industry, where certain types of workers stay at home and use computer/communications equipment to perform job tasks and to maintain links with the office. This saves on the need for office space in a centralized location, cuts down on commuting time, and provides a sometimes "better" way of life. It also once again leads to a break down in traditional loyalties to the employer and to one's fellow worker. Maintenance of a system for protection of proprietary information which depends upon these bonds becomes increasingly difficult for the security practitioner.

Summary

We must recognize these trends as important to our planning. They are not inevitable in all their described detail but awareness provides a reasonable structure to our thinking for the future. What conclusions can we draw from our discussion of these three megatrends and how should the security professional prepare? First, the future as we move into the information age is built around the microchip. Security practitioners, if they have any hope to have any relevancy to the real world, must be familiar with application and security implications of computing systems.

A second conclusion which we can identify is that the security professional must integrate himself into the selection process of computer systems to ensure that proper security is built into the systems at the start. Retroactive security measures are always cumbersome, not particularly effective, and expensive. Early security integration into the systems process also allows preimplementation employees orientation concerning security needs. All protective systems are vulnerable to human error, undisciplined usage, and of course, actual malfeasance. There is no indication at present that future practical business security systems for mass use will not be vulnerable to human factors. An informed, cooperative work force with a good knowledge of the company's standards of ethics will continue to be the best security system available.

The security manager is not responsible for the general mores of the culture in which he lives. However, he is responsible for aid in design and implementation of security methods based on the human factors which will make security reasonable from the perspectives of business and people. While the security manager cannot be expected to design computer security equipment or software, he can play a critical role in their development, selection, and application. It is necessary only that the security manager set general standards of security for equipment to be purchased and then encourage the procurement activities to meet specifications.

The professional security manager must have an understanding of the developing business and societal environment in the information age. Included in this understanding must be a capability to deal knowledgeably with technological security issues. By being well prepared to deal with the information issues which will become important and aggressively pursing the right goals through professionally prepared recommendations on technology issues, the security manager will be brought into management circles as senior management recognizes the importance of the information resource. He or she will be asked to participate in decision processes, rather than being on the trailing edge of business decisions.

Finally, today's security manager must do those things, and have those skills, which will cause him or her to be viewed as an essential part of the "management team." As competition increases and the information resource becomes ever more important, businesses will need good security. In fact, considering that information is THE critical resource for the information age, an effective program for information security becomes a critical management task. The security professional must be aware of these developing trends, capable of making informed judgements and providing expert advice on technology-related issues; further, he/she must step forward aggressively to propose innovative solutions which meet the requirements of changing times.

7

Security — Contribution to Corporate Profits

Clay E. Higgins, CPP

Project Manager-Security
NUS Corporation
Gaithersburg, Maryland

"Our best thought comes from others."
EMERSON

Within the last 40 years, according to "The Task Force on Private Security" published by the Department of Justice in 1976, the private security industry has been visualized as offering deadend careers, with duties performed by personnel characterized as the unemployable. The security image was that of an elderly, sloppily uniformed man asleep in a gate house. The security representative was the corporate cop. Needless to say, the security industry has had a hard time overcoming that early image.

In the past 10 years, security management concepts concentrated on finding a corporate security executive (manager) and getting away from the corporate cop. The modern security manager's job is increasingly complex, and requires the security manager to deal with all levels of employees and sophisticated problems from personnel matters to criminal investigations to computer electronics. The image of the security department has improved partly from hard work and partly from the realzation that security costs have risen to over $40 billion yearly and theft costs are triple that amount.

Today, the security manager is projected as an executive, but security is still guards, gatehouses, fences, locks, electronic gadgets, gongs, whistles, cameras, and lighting. How do we improve the security department to match the executive image? How do we stop theft in this era of a "rip-off" society and lenient authorities when our present guard programs do not seem to stop the steady increase in the national crime statistics for businesses?

Guard personnel are still considered marginal personnel with little or no career opportunities and the position is characterized by low salaries, high personnel turnover, little or no training, and ineffective performance. With this in mind, what is the direction for the modern corporate securty department? There are many unanswered questions, but the future seems to be in total corporate commitment to reduction of all losses through management of the various security programs. The security department must become the loss prevention department and must escape the sterotyped guard image established by the security industry 40 years ago.

To make this escape into the future, the practice of hiring former heads of police, FBI, etc. organizations directly into top security positions must stop. Security and public law enforcement are separate fields and with different orientations. Former public law enforcement officers need three to five years security experience to transition into an executive position within security. I have yet to talk to a former FBI or police official who did not admit (in private conversation) that their former work did not prepare them for a job as Director of Security. They learned their new work through on-the-job training and at the expense of their employer. In many cases, this meant that the subordinates had to train the boss, which is counter-productive and detracts from employee morale.

The future in security is not headed toward more arrests and convictions of bandits, muggers and hit-and-run "rip-off" artists. An arrest, by a security person, without the presence of a court-order and a public peace officer, will be a thing of the past. The establishment of crime prevention programs, their supervision and management and the overall success of these program's abilities to reduce *all* losses, will be the benchmark security directors will be rated against.

In a magazine article by a national publication, a senior police official stated that he was worried about the rise of non-public law enforcement types in security because, as he stated, "I hope they know enough to make an arrest." My reply to that is, "I hope they don't." Security is not there to take over the job of public police. I just hope public police officials, when they enter security, will be able to stop internal theft, frauds, and thousands of flim-flams committed against employers on a daily basis by employees and costing over $90 billion yearly. These are little crimes that public police have no time for, but literally mean life or death for America's corporations.

Maintenance of profits in the 1900's

The goal for the 1990's is to transition past the corporate cop image and establish a well managed and respected security organization within your corporate structure.

The objectives that must be accomplished to reach that goal are:
1. Establish security as a reorganized career field.
2. The security department must effectively reduce losses and crime.
3. Security must become involved with all losses within the corporation, not just a uniformed guard and alarm department.
4. Security must take the lead, and be imaginative and innovative in its implementation of security measures.
5. Security must become as much of an integral part of the organization as the personnel, purchasing, accounting, etc. departments.

To accomplish these goals and objectives, the security manager must develop a well organized and sophisticated organization. The *hardest job* facing the security manager in the 1990's is learning to work within the corporate structure and to receive support for and implementation of security goals and objectives.

Security department management in the future must contribute to the corporate bottom line — profits. Corporate security must be managed with loss prevention as its major concern, because this directly affects profits; security must be considered as an investment in avoiding losses and recovering assets. To accomplish this contribution to the bottom line, security must be totally integrated into the corporate planning base and receive top management's support. This necessary support starts with corporate management's understanding of how security contributes.

The sophistication of today's crime and/or lack of employee honesty demands that security professionals proceed past the traditional concepts of security into the total security concept of loss prevention. Security professionals can and will reduce losses if they organize and manage corporate security with a management system. To accomplish this goal, the security manager must mobilize the entire corporation into thinking loss prevention and understanding of each employee's responsibility to reduce losses. The security manager becomes the corporate consultant on security and advises and assists the various locations and departments in the implementation phases. Through the awareness programs developed and implemented by the security director, reduction or theft (employee and outsiders) is achieved.

Corporate losses have been estimated at about $100 billion yearly and will triple by 1990. If a corporation states it is not suffering losses - either losses and/or thefts (e.g., inventory shrinkage, employee time card fraud, etc.), then these losses are not being identified as losses or the company has not recognized that these losses are real and affect company profits. The corporate security management program must be a series of security sub-systems designed for total loss prevention and security of personnel, property, and information. This demands that the security management system designed for a complex must consider losses avoided or assets recovered through proper employment of security methods and means to compute the payback for the security dollar invested.

The structuring of the security management systems is important and must address several considerations. The first consideration is to avoid the "fortress syndrome"; security programs are not just guards and alarms. The best security is aware corporate employees. Design the entire corporate security programs, starting with corporate policy, to meet the real threat — the insider as well as the intruder. The next consideration is to implement the corporate security policy by getting policy properly approved and incorporated into the appropriate corporate policy and procedures. The final step is to establish a system to implement the corporate policy into standards and procedures to be used by the security department, middle management, operating staff, and line-employees in the performance of every-day duties. Emphasis must be established that security is each employee's business, not only limited to the security department. Each level of management and supervision must be encouraged to accept its security responsibilities and to implement security within its areas of influence.

Corporate loss prevention should be addressed as part of the overall corporate policy. This should include designation of security responsibilities and establishment of a security organization. Corporate standards should be developed for everyday use by all management levels within the company. These corporate standards should provide direction to establish security management sub-systems, designate minimum acceptable standards of performance, and establish a security department to overall security related matters. The standards should be formalized by procedures required to implement and promulgae corporate standards into instructions and guidelines for all levels of personnel within the company.

It is important to evaluate how these systems contribute to security management and corporate profit. The evaluation is not easy, but profit is the goal. To reach that goal requires establishment of a formal program and a willingness to fully implement the system. It is then necessary to monitor the system to ensure compliance and achievement of desired results.

Each system must be expanded and developed into detailed standards and procedures useful for daily application by the end users. (Another name for each security system is security program.) Envision corporate policy as a pyramid.

Policy is developed and approved at the senior management level, at the top of the pyramid. This covers the top third of the corporation, but only a small number of personnel.

Standards are designed for middle management (both security and operating staff) to ensure that managers have direction on all security matters. This is the middle third of the pyramid; however, it covers a larger group of personnel than the top, but is still limited to a select group.

Procedures are the details used by the operating staff and end user and is functional or site specific. This is the bottom third of the pyramid and the largest group of personnel affected.

Lastly, the security manager of the 1990's must implement the corporate security policy. (As we know, getting policy in writing and signed is not the same as implementation.) The recommended implementation method is to train all employees through a formal security awareness program. However, the key to the implementation is to require the support of - and the classroom attendance of-corporate managers and directors, followed by department heads and line-supervisors, and lastly the rank and file.

Each level of management and supervision will (wear the additional hat of security supervisor) have distinct security responsibilities, and will act as an extension of the Corporate Security program. Security, incorporated within all levels of management and supervision, will relieve the coporation of the need for additional and costly security personnel and equipment. Remember, the best security obtainable is aware and responsible employees.

With today's sophistication and complexity of crime, a total security program as described above may be a corporation's only means of self-defense in this world of stiff competition, mobile employees, and lack of loyalty to the Company paying the weekly salaries.

Security as Managed in the Year 2000

Security in the year 2000 will see the corporate security/loss prevention director as the principle advisor to the corporation for all matters relating to loss vulnerabilities and associated risks. The success of the plant/department manager in the year 2000 will depend on the security department's ability to reduce crime and losses through elimination of excessive scraps, reduction of sales frauds, eliminate collusion in purchasing and accounting, and the ability to motivate employees, through security awareness, to reduce internal shrinkage, pilferage, and false insurance and health claims. This broad scope of responsibilities must be the result of effective management systems.

With the steady rise of crime and its complexities, do not be suprised to see Corporate Security elevated to a principal staff position reporting directly to the CEO or the President.

An effective total coporate security management system may feature some of the following sub-systems:

1. Corporate Security and Loss Prevention System
2. Proprietary Information and Document Control System
3. Inventory and Property Control System
4. Shipping and Receiving System
5. Security (Guard) Force System
6. System for maintaining External Services
7. Employee and Visitor Controls/Badging System
8. Alarms and Monitoring System
9. Computer Security System
10. Loss Reporting System
11. Executive Protection System
12. Employee Security Awareness System
13. Industrial Emergency Planning System
14. Fire/Safety System
15. Liability Insurance Loss System

A brief Summation of these sub-systems are all that space permits.

Corporate Security Management Systems

Electronics will revolutionize security management. Security MIS (Management Information Systems) will be tied in (on-line) with all functions within the plant. Terminals will automatically notify security of new-hires, personnel terminations, training, clearances, education, as well as tracking for document controls, warehousing, purchasing, receiving, payables, insurance claims, fire/safety audits and updates. Methods will be available to track sales, and correlate with production and warehousing to prevent fraud in operations.

Access controls will provide for employee time and attendance, visitor control and provide automated payrolls and audit features. Electronics will also provide for sophisticated security features as discussed below.

Security Department

The organization corporate security department will have a full-time professional Corporate Security/Loss Prevention Director. The security department charter is to conduct loss prevention programs and reports to a level within the organization that is above the line departments and plant management staffs. This is necessary as security must work across deparmental lines to accomplish its many responsibilities.

The security department will be headed by a professional from the private security sector. Private security (utilities or industrial) orientation is in the crime prevention mode, and can contribute most successfully when allowed to prevent crime. Public law enforcement is oriented to identify and prosecute criminals after the crime has been committed. Using the old philosophy "an ounce of prevention is worth a pound of cure," there must be concentration on prevention, not prosecution of crime.

The security department's charter includes provisions to have the security director's review and approval of all the security effort within the corporation, e.g. guard contracts, alarm systems, locking and key controls, security auditing, computer programs, employee screening, investigations, and police liaison. The security department is used as a corporate security consultant to improve profits at all management levels and locations. In addition, the security director has direct inputs to all areas where profit can be improved by reduction of loss.

PROPRIETARY INFORMATION AND DOCUMENT CONTROL SYSTEM

Methods for implementation of proprietary security and document control are the use of non-disclosure agreements, employment contracts, and the security awareness program discussed later. The methods also apply to computer security requirements. All persons are required to receive initial training and retraining on information control. All documents will be numbered and computerized. Whether a corporation shows a profit or a loss can depend on its success in protecting proprietary information which accounts for 85% of white collar crime.

INVENTORY AND PROPERTY CONTROL SYSTEM

Inventory controls are applicable to fixed assets, logistics stocks, and software library. These assets will be computerized and subject to continuous audit. Responsible individuals are assigned all assets.

Checks and balances are added to ensure shipping, warehousing, and operations inventories agree. The losses sustained in all of the above can seriously affect employee morale, cause delays in delivery, set back operations schedules, and result in lost sales. The security department investigations section will follow-up on all reports of inventory loss, not only to recover the material and reveal the guilty, but more importantly to determine countermeasures that will prevent recurrence.

SHIPPING AND RECEIVING SYSTEM

Procedures are established to ensure that incoming or outgoing deliveries are not left unsecured and easily pilfered. Accounting procedures are established to check items against bills of lading to ensure receipt, in good order, of all goods delivered. In addition, a supervised double-count system is established to insure outgoing shipments do not contain more items than listed on the manifest.

Purchsing, receiving, and the warehousing functions will be separate and all three should remain separate from the accounts payable function, to reduce fraud potential. The purpose of the separate functions is to assist in the avoidance of collusion between insiders as well as external persons which can cost the company millions in shipping, receiving, and purchasing. The security department investigation section supplies a loss prevention specialist to corporate audit teams auditing these functions. In addition, security will provide continuous audit by its computer terminals.

SECURTIY (GUARD) FORCE

The security force is an essential component of the security system. Traditional duties of a guard are no longer applicable. Security loss prevention function is performed by highly skilled auditors and investigators. The physical security specialists will replace the shift guard. This physical security specialist will be responsible for the physical aspects of security at the plant (e.g., patrolling, key rounds, fire/safety, etc).

Generally speaking, guard personnel will be held to a minimum, while using security electronics, equipment, security awareness programs, security compliance audits, and the operating managment staff to the maximum. Guard salaries are the most expensive part of security operations, hence justifying considerable attention to achieving the desired effectiveness with the least number of people.

SYSTEMS FOR MAINTAINING EXTERNAL SERVICES

External services include maintenance and cleaning vendors, courier services, delivery services, office equipment maintenance services, security services contractors, lessor agents or representatives, contract employees, and utility and telephone employees. Outsiders are badged, logged into the access control computer, escorted and limited to those areas clearly required by their service. Security checks are made of vendor's reliability, integrity, employee turnover experience, supervision, selection of its own employees, and whether the facility has the same crew or individual(s) on a routine basis.

The security department investigations section conduct or assist in the conduct of vendor evaluation checks. External services employees are a prime source of inventory theft and loss of proprietary information.

EMPLOYEE VISITOR CONTROLS/BADGING SYSTEM

In an effort to maintain an environment conducive to good work habits, as well as to provide basic security, control of employees and visitors is necessary. Employee identification is necessary to ensure the person is an employee and is authorized into a particular work area. Lastly, visitor badging discourages vagrants from wandering in "off-the-street." It also discourages insurance salesmen, charity drives, etc., from disrupting work. Family and friends visiting during work hours are discouraged.

Lost work time costs money. Vendors (insurance salesmen, encyclopedia salesmen, etc.) going directly to the employees' work areas can be highly disruptive to good work habits. Additionally, uncontrolled visitors are a good example of how proprietary information is stolen. The end result is loss of corporate profits.

ALARM AND MONITORING SYSTEMS

Strategically placed redundant alarm systems that are properly monitored and supervised assist greatly in the physical protection of company assets, either property or information. Security alarm systems reduce overall security costs and also deny unauthorized persons from access to sensitive areas. Alarm systems cost between $0.75 to $1.00 an hour after installation versus $7.50 (an hour upward) for guards. The security systems extends the guard force's capability and adds "cost-effective" eyes and ears to the security program. Closed circuit television with video tape recording capability allows security to access alarms, identify authorized persons, and to replace the need for guard personnel at key stations.

However, the physical security aspects are overridden by the criticalness of internal controls such as documentation controls, magnetic media controls, redundant records, segregation of duties, and the interface with other corporate functions. The security department heads a team from the personnel department, internal audit, accounting and finance, legal and the computer department management which is committed to security principles. This effort alone maintains survivability of the coporation as computer privacy reaches almost unfathomable penetration in the work of electronics by the year 2000.

LOSS REPORTING SYSTEM

All real or suspected losses are reported to corporate security for appropriate follow-up action. Not all losses (in some cases the majority) are attributable to a criminal act. However, shipping errors, damage, poor inventory controls, shrinkage, and a variety of other circumstances can lead to a "loss." Proper follow-up investigation, remedial actions, as well as continuous auditing procedures significantly reduce opportunity for these events to occur. The main goal is to improve the system to preclude recurrence. Recovery of goods and catching the thief is surely a means to that end. Appropriate means are made to protect stock and warehouse items during off-peak times (night-weekends-holidays). A loss reporting system can effectively reduce shrinkage losses and therefore add to corporate profit. The security department investigation section shall be the prime mover of this system.

EXECUTIVE PROTECTION SYSTEM

Executive protection has become a major item of concern, nationally as well as internationally. Terrorist acts, extortion, and other acts long associated with overseas activity has come to the United States. All that is necessary to be a target of these acts is to be a corporate executive who is perceived to have money available to him/her. The next vulnerability is an executive of a corporation that is the target for "media events"; e.g., demonstrations to get attention, or extortion to gain a forum to make a statement. The executive victim may or may not be directly connected to the exact target within the corporation.

Cost of insurances, bodyguards, ransom payments, etc. sometimes are only a small part of the overall cost to the corporation in adverse publicity and lost services.

EMPLOYEE SECURITY AWARENESS SYSTEM

All employees are required to attend training to be made aware of their individual security responsibilities. This awareness includes three areas: personal security, security of property, and information security. A continuous program is established to brief all employees, followed by new employee security orientation, and a continuing security education program for all employees. A solid line of security guards around the perimeter of the property cannot ensure security unless all employees are aware of their individual roles in loss prevention are complying with security directives. The corporation is prepared to enforce security rules.

An alert and vigilant staff will contribute significant dollars to the corporate profits in terms of losses prevented. The corporate director of security should direct and coordinate the security awareness program; however, all level of management and supervision must be mobilized to ensure compliance by all personnel for maximum effectiveness.

INDUSTRIAL EMERGENCY PLANNING SYSTEM

The industrial emergency plan contributes to loss reduction during and following emergency situations. Areas covered in the emergency plan include fire/safety, bomb threats, hostage/extortion, riots, demonstrations, strikes, flooding or water damage, and acts of God (hurricane, storms). Business interruption and loss of office/operation space planning is considered also.

The emergency plan is a cost effective alternative to bankruptcy. The seriousness of domestic security emergencies and the importance of economic recovery after a major disaster/emergency is of national concern.

Each facility has an up-to-date emergency plan and is organized with a formalized chain of command to deal with emergencies that may occur.

FIRE/SAFETY SYSTEM

The fire/safety system plan is incorporated into each facility as both part of the Industrial Emergency Plan and the Employee Awareness System. Instructions are posted and the plan is practiced. A well organized and praticed fire/safety plan reduces loss during and after a fire. Insurance premiums are geared to adequacy of fire systems, and a well practiced and workable plan helps hold down the cost of insurance.

LIABILITY INSURANCE LOSS SYSTEM

Industrial safety and workers' compensation are considered as part of the safety system. This area handles OSHA concerns, industrial safety, fire codes, and investigations of injuries and workers' compensation claims. Workers' compensation fraud against employers is increasingly costly to business. Fraudulent claims over $40,000 a year per person have been recorded within Massachusetts. Reducing these claims saves dollars to be invested for business. Other risk management techniques applied to all areas of liability insurance can assist in holding down insurance costs, penalties, and legal fees. The security department actively investigates and documents all accidents and claims that may or may not result in cost to the corporation.

CONCLUSIONS

Properly applied corporate security in the year 2000 more than pays for itself through reduction of loss through awareness. Although the visible aspects of security (guards, barriers, and alarms, etc.) is still seen as a cost, the greater savings are through loss reduction and assets recovery. Reduction of losses is accomplished through integration of security provisions and attitudes with other company operations, as a management principle, to be implemented from the top down. Thus, the key person on the management team is the security manager who must implement the integrated security program.

The management systems described above may not be the answer to all security problems of the year 2000. They are, however, a good place to start. Security management systems are tailored to site-specific considerations to properly protect the type of business, product, and environment in which the business operates. To accomplish the ambitious security program as described above requires an active security manager, experienced in industrial security, with an understanding of business. The security manager must be able to write, conceptualize, and implement corporate policy. Most of all, the security director must be able to meet the corporate officers and managers on an equal level to sell the security programs and to be accepted as a security executive and not the corporate cop.

RECOMMENDATIONS

Security is a very broad responsibility and will have to receive attention and awareness at the highest levels of management. Some recommendations to ensure the security department is properly managed to meet the challenge of tomorrow are as follows:

- Acquire a security consultant or a security manager with excellent credentials in industrial security to establish and implement the security program.
- Establish high level management support to eliminate the corporate cop concept.
- Establish the security department with a charter to advise and consult on all security matters at all locations and in all departments.
- Ensure the security charter contains policy that allows the security department to investigate all losses from all locations.
- Establish security programs within the organization that are comprehensive, yet written in a language that is useful and available to all.
- Establish a security awareness program for all employees.
- Be prepared to enforce security rules.

Corporate security is as necessary and essential to business profitability as production, marketing, purchasing, personnel, legal, and financial functions. In the year 2000, security may be the critical ingredient that dictates corporate survival versus extinction.

Clay Higgins was the supervisor of a security consulting and engineering group within a major multi-national firm and is a longterm member of the ASIS Physical Security Committee.

8

International Security Management in the Year 2000

George W. Ryan, C.P.P.

"Terrorists are now more willing to attack persons instead of property. The increased security around facilities has also encouraged them to attack a soft target — people."

BRIAN M. JENKINS

The security manager of national and multinational companies of today must prepare themselves professionally for the challenges of the 21st century. In just a few short years the year 2000 will arrive, and with it all scientific advances and fantastic international affairs' changes that one can hardly imagine. There is a great deal of mysticism attached to the year 2000, as if it will mark the turn of not only the century, but of the way people will live, work, and deal with the world and space from then on. The security manager of today must look to the year 2000 and beyond and attempt to identify all the changes in his profession that time will bring. He must examine the way business, industry, politics and, in general, the worldwide dynamics which are so much influencing every aspect of life as we know it today.

The security profession has undergone considerable change in the past several decades, and it will undergo even greater changes in the future. To attempt to better understand the future trends and dynamic influences affecting the security profession, it is worthwhile if one looks first at the past.

When World War II ended in 1945, reconstruction of the Western-World's industrial system and its production facilities was identified as the most important objective to be accomplished in the post-war years. The United States had not suffered any particular damage to its industrial complex during the war, and the conversion from a wartime to a peace-time production system was accomplished in a short period of time. With the Marshall Plan, U.S. business and industry were able to assist in the establishment and construction of production facilities in Europe. With a booming economy and a fast growing export business, the United States rapidly expanded its worldwide business complex through multinational companies, doing business in many countries. The ownership, management and technical operations of most of these companies were almost entirely American. Foreign nationals in the various countries where these companies were doing business were normally engaged to handle lower level positions and to work in the plants, in the factories or on construction projects, as the case might have been. The rapid growth in the United States in research and development in the fields of technology, science, medicine, computers, space exploration, military weaponry and in many aspects of services and systems, attracted not only the best of our own talents in these various fields, but it also attracted the talent from many countries around the world. Many millions of dollars were invested in a multitude of research and development projects, with the latest facilities equipment, materials and research data coming together and being made available to this growing pool of intellectual pioneers. The money to finance these projects was available to this growing pool of intellectual pioneers. The money to finance these projects was available in the U.S. The phenomena of all these people going to America to carry out their research, experimentation and development of technology and products, was referred to as the Brain Drain. It gave the United States a tremendous advantage in many fields of enterprise and in many scientific disciplines. Much of the resulting technology from this massive research and development movement was considered to be classified by the U.S. government because of the military potential involved or the commercial value they represented. The need to safeguard the Research and Development facilities, the projects being carried out, and the resultant technological developments from unauthorized access, or from misuse or abuse by anyone having knowledge of them, became more and more apparent to the Industrial Complex management dealing with these matters. Many of the companies involved were already dealing with the United States government and were thus guided in their corporate security systems management by practices and procedures established by the Department of Defense (DOD). These companies carried out their security responsibilities under the general supervision of DOD, and were able to minimize the security weaknesses and exposures which were often found in non-defense related businesses and industries. The private industrial sector research and development in such areas as electronics, computer software and hardware, pharmaceuticals, genetic engineering, and medicine also had need of security management and security systems which would protect their technology and products development from falling into unauthorized hands. Competition in the business world has placed tremendous competitive pressures on these companies to remain on the leading edge of the hi-technology expansion. Any company which does not do so will soon find its position in the market to be in jeopardy. The planning and programming organizations of all successful companies are looking far ahead. With the advent of successful recovery from damages of World War II to their industrial manufacturing and production complexes, such countries as Britain, France, Japan and Germany also began to make significant strides in their technological research and development programs, and began attracting their scientists back to their own laboratories. Many millions of dollars were, and are being invested by these countries to develop new products which will compete favorably, or exclusively in the world. The results have been dramatic. We have witnessed a very substantial swing in the international industrial production patterns, from "Made in the USA," to "Made in the USA, Japan, German, Britain, etc." Multinational companies which were almost a monopoly of American business, have now been joined by multinational companies from almost every other industrial nation. In the automobile industry for example, parts manufacturing plants are located in many different countries — usually where large markets exist and where labor costs are low. Assembly plants are also located near the markets, and many people from many nationalities and backgrounds are now involved in the production, marketing, maintenance and management of all multinational companies. More recently, with increased competition, increased costs recessions in different countries, and with the recognition that survival requires international realignment, both the style of these companies, their organizations, their business concepts, their ownerships, their managements and virtually their entire structures, have moved from a multinational to an international status. Now that we have considered some of the evolutionary trends affecting the move from multinational to international business and industry, let us consider what impact these have had and will have on the role and activities of the security function in the multinational company of today and the international company of the future.

Management of the security function in business and industry has developed into a profession which is being increasingly recognized and respected by management of business and industry. For many years during the evolutionary growth of the American industrial complex, the security responsibilities were being carried out by people who had either retired from law enforcement agencies, military organizations, or merely gravitated to this field of endeavor through chance or fate. The knowledge of industrial security which was possessed by many of the security practitioners was limited to guard work or police-related duties. Most businesses regarded the security group as a guard force, where any employee could be relegated when he ceased to function effectively in other areas of the company. Very often men who had suffered industrial injuries and who could no longer perform their normal job were placed in a uniform, at a gate to look at cars and people entering or leaving a plant facility. The security activities of companies, almost without exception, were considered as *cost centers,* rather than as *profit centers.* Management looked upon the security activity as a necessary evil, and as a drain on operating funds. Whenever the head of the security organization would submit his budget to management for the next operating year, he would find the competition from other organizations in the company for every available budget dollar to be very strong and most often security would lose out. Very often when cuts in the budget would be imposed, the security organization could be one of the first to be cut back. That represented a "savings" to the uninformed, unaware managements of the past and, in too many instances, of the present as well. These cuts in security only served to expose the company's assets to greater losses. Over the years from within the ranks of professional security managers, there began to emerge numerous security business executives. One must accept that there is a great difference in professional thrust between a security manager, who supervises the affairs of a company's local security activities, and the security business executive who plans, develops and implements all of a company's international security programs, and who becomes part of the company's executive management team. He is the security executive who looks at the future and identifies the direction his company's security activities must take. He knows the company's future plans and gears the security program to them. The *international* security executive is beginning to emerge in the security profession. He is a professional who has worked in international security affairs, has become academically qualified and who through his growth as a security professional has become part of the management team. His efforts are directed toward the multitude of problems one finds in international operations and his contribution to an international company's profitability is both expected and recognized. He is a professional who has reached his executive level because he has been able to demonstrate to his management that he not only produces excellent security for the company, but that he does so as a part of their team, and effects a strong impact on profits through his programs. He has succeeded in making his management "aware" of the value of security to the *bottom line* figure which all businesses strive for — increased yield on investment — i.e., *profits.* The Security business executive of today must not only understand the business of security in virtually all of its ramifications, but he must also understand the overall operations, organization, politics, plans and economics of the enterprise which employs him. He must be a student of foreign affairs, different cultures,languages and culture influences. Only by remaining up-to-date on the most recent advances and developments (state of the art) in the many aspects of the security business can a security man truly think of himself as a professional, and thus remain equal to the challenges the changing world of criminals, terrorists, and international industrial espionage agents pose for him. The evolution of the multinational companies into international companies is bringing with it the need for international security management which will be trained and experienced to respond to the security requirements inherent in such worldwide movements. Each security management professional is well advised to take stock of the existing security posture in the company he works for. He should look back over the past ten or fifteen years and examine the progress his company had made, and how it has grown and expanded. He should also examine what impact these changes have had upon the security activity. An understanding of the past, a very accurate knowledge of the present, and a clear plan, with objectives, for the near-term and long-term, will permit the security business executive to serve his employer effectively and efficiently.

As one looks at the business and industrial world of today, with its technological explosions rocking the way businesses were conducted in the past, one can realize that such things as computers and computer software hold many keys to the advances mankind will make in just a few short years from now. The security business executive who recognizes the role that computers are already playing in the multinational and international companies will quickly note that the security profession must hasten to make equal technological progress, or it will be left behind, and thus placed in jeopardy of being out-of-date and inadequate. The security manager who makes it his goal to learn *now,* all he can about the computer world, its value to his company as a business tool and its value to him as a security professional, will be the security business executive who prepares himself to meet the security-related challenges of the 21st century.

In the past number of years we have seen men land on the moon; we have sent space ships out into infinity; taking space photos and electronically transmitting computer print-out imagery of other distant planets and their moons. We are sending more and more satellites into orbit around the earth, and conducting many experiments in space, to study the impact of space on such scientific projects as are sent, and thus seeking ways to improve the quality of life on earth. We are seeing the phenomenal advances in genetic engineering, gene splicing, recombinant engineering, i.e., the stuff of which life itself is made. Scientific minds are leading us into the unknown at an ever-increasing rate, and the billions of people on earth are to be the beneficiaries and/or the victims of these scientific developments. With the improvements in science, technology and products resulting from these scientific discoveries, our world is being reached in every area, and seems to be shrinking. Certainly, from a relative point of view, it is smaller in the reduced time required for travel (once around the world in one hour). Communications are instantaneous. particularly in the reporting of world events as they occur. Television, radio newspapers, and other worldwide media and communications systems provide up-to-the-minute facts and information of what is taking place anywhere in, around or near our world. How does all of this relate to the security profession, one might ask? One response might be that people will always want to feel secure in whatever environment develops. Another might be that the security business must move into the space age too. Nations, governments, companies, industries and all mankind want to feel safe and secure within their borders and extraterritorially as well. Making the world safe is certainly fraught with complex problems, noting the nuclear, missile and military readiness of many nations. However, it is in that kind of complexity that the challenges lie for truly professional international security management. International companies have today, and will have increasing business activities in more and more areas of the world in the future. Security professionals must prepare now for the future. This can be done by conducting a survey of the influences and dynamics of the world business and industrial environment on their company's and their own security posture. In trying to determine whether you have thought about or planned for a position in the international security profession of the future, ask yourself such questions as the following:

1. How many foreign languages do you speak?
2. How many different countries have you visited?
3. In how many countries does your company operate?
4. How well do you know where different countries are located, the names of their capital cities, the names of the President, King, Sheikh or Emir.
5. What do you know about Capitalism or Communism?
6. What do you know of the cultures, customs, mores or histories of other countries?
7. How well versed are you on world politics?
8. How well do you understand other systems of government, and economic influences on them?
9. What have you done in the last five years to improve your professional stature? What are your plans for the next five years in this regard? Does your management look to you to safeguard their future.
10. Are you part of your company's management team?
11. Can you respond technically to the security challenges posed by the changes in business systems?
12. Are you a *Cost* Center or Profit Center?
13. What studying have you done, or do you do to try to remain current with the fast moving trends of your company's business? or your own profession? of world affairs?
14. Are you familiar with the computer environment in your company?
15. Do you operate a computer terminal?
16. Do you own a personal computer?
17. Have you developed a computer security management plan for your company? Have you conducted a computer security survey?

18. Have you developed a security management program for your security program?
19. Have you convinced your management of the profitability of an effective computer security program and had them issue a computer security policy statement?
20. Are your computers, computer data and all the related environment protected by a comprehensive disaster and recovery plan?

These and many other questions when asked and answered will help you better understand where you stand today as a responsible, effective security professional.

The following matrix identifies certain specific points which have direct impact and implications upon the evolutionary changes which have, are, and will take place in corporate security. The matrix covers the periods pre-World War II, World War II to the present, and present to 2000 and beyond. First, use the matrix to examine the subject matters which have been selected as they apply to your own experiences and your present security position.

CORPORATE SECURITY IMPLICATIONS OF CHANGE

Dynamic subjects have impact, implications upon Corporate Security	Prior to W W II	WWII to present	Present to 2000 and beyond
Nature of Industry/ Business	Materials Intensive	Machine Intensive	People Intensive
Communications	Verbal	Paper	Electronic
Financial Media	Cash	Checks	EFT - Electronic Funds Transfer
Geographic Corporate Focus	European changing to U.S. based	U.S. based changing to multinational	Multinational changing to international
Legal Emphasis	Local	National	International
Travel	Minimum	Extensive	Moderate to extensive (Effect of improvement in communication will be offset by international expansion)
Employee Motivative	Goal Oriented	Role Oriented	Quality of life Oriented
Biggest Threats	Theft	Carlessness	Terrorism, Political Activism
Security Orientation Emphasis	Direct Observation	Technical	Theoretical Management
Potential Disruption	Internal	Local	Worldwide
Deterrence Role	Reactive	Proactive & Reactive	Redesign of Environment
Security Functional Role	Cost Center	Cost Center Changing to Profit Center	Profit Center changing to Integrated Service Center
Background of Security Personnel	Chosen for physical size or Company Loyalty	Ex-law Enforcement or military	Professionally Educated
Education of Security Personnel	No Special Requirements	High School to College Grad.	College Graduate to Post Grad. Education
Security Goals	Prevention or Disruption of Loss	Loss Prevention and Legal Requirements	Business Integrity
Security Tools	Direct Observation	Paper Work	Computerized Models

Examine these also as they might apply to the company by whom you are employed. Notice the significant changes which have already taken place and how your present security role and the environment in which you work are undergoing constant change. You will readily see by looking at the matrix as a whole that the changes shown from the Nature of Industry and Business down to the Security Tools required to keep up with these changes, that the security professional must expand from a parochial local, limited individual, to one who anticipates the changes set forth in each topic listed on the matrix and who begins planning today for the year 2000 and beyond. By establishing clear objectives for the 1990's, one can work toward meeting these and be well on the way to being prepared for whatever the year 2000 may bring. The international companies require international security executives who not only understand these dynamic trends, but who have made it their goal to be equal to the challenges of the world of international affairs. There is much travel involved dealing in international affairs and the security responsibilities will require a considerable amount of it. The security executive will develop his contacts and security resources in the areas where his company work will send him and he will be able to function much in the same manner he did when he was responsible only for local security matters. The matrix will provide you with some interesting, thought provoking ideas about the world of the future, and as you develop each point in its meaning to you as a security professional, you will certainly find additional topics which you can add to the list which will influence the future trends and impacts upon corporate security in the international mode. When one becomes part of the international security profession one enjoys the marvelous opportunities of meeting security representatives from other countries in their environments. The experiences that come from dealing in international security-related matters are considerable. The need for diplomacy and tact when interfacing with people in the many countries of the world becomes recognized more and more with each contact. If one has developed his professional skills along the lines set forth by the matrix, the international security executive of the 1990's, the year 2000 and beyond will find his financial compensation to be substantially more than it might have been had he not done so. The demands on the security profession will be considerable and the value to the international companies of the truly competent professional will also be considerable. American business and industry will remain the leader of the free world in the Space Age, as it has been since World War II.

Space Age security is at hand. Space Age security professionals must prepare now. The international security manager of the Year 2000 may be you if you are prepared. If you are not, it will surely be the man who is. There's not much time left — use it wisely and protect your future. Become a 2000 man today; the future is now.

9

Crime Prevention Techniques in the United Kingdom in the Year 2000 A.D.

Mervyn Bowden, BA, Churchill Fellow 1981

South Wales Constabulary, Police Headquarters, Bridgend,
Mid Glamorgan, CF31 3SU, South Wales, Great Britain

"Positive attitude breeds confidence and enthusiasm."
DR. CHARLES M. GIRARD

Societies are totally dependent on the physical environment they occupy. An environment will eventually impose conditions and restrictions on, and finally pressures against, the growth of the society it hosts. The social system is finely balanced to cope with external pressures and, at its optimum level of efficiency, will have developed such an intricacy and sophistication that it is the collective awareness of its participants that maintains the balance which keeps it a viable alternative to anarchy.

The danger for any society is that it can run too well. If it provides the atmosphere for optimum physical growth and intellectual development for too long a period, that growth and development may increase at a rate not proportional to society's ability to cope with it.

Our society is already under such pressure that radical change is becoming almost inevitable. The physical and intellectual growth of the human race is now increasing so quickly that society is becoming blase about its achievements, but bewildered by its failings. When technical developments of the most complex kind are everyday occurrences, when violence which would have caused public uproar even a century ago becomes not only accepted but expected, and when the termination of the human race is no longer science fiction but a recognised possibility, the risk is that people will begin to feel their own and society's future is hopeless. A sense of futility which is fatal to any organised, self-motivating social system could easily pervade society.

In this instance it becomes necessary to view anti-social behaviour as a symptom of a threatened society rather than as some kind of disease. Crime is a long established human activity. Although never eradicated completely, it has been kept under control largely because, although not acceptable to the majority, its motives have usually been recognisable, purposeful and in some ways, logical. Crime would therefore be prevented, investigated or punished because — in however perverted a way — criminals played by the rules imposed upon them by society.

The increase in extreme anti-social behaviour, on the other hand, is characterised by its excessive violence and apparent lack of motive or provocation. Although the perpetrator is striking out against society, it is the individual who necessarily becomes the victim.

If we are to protect ourselves both as individuals and as a society, we must realise that while we can deal with traditional crime using established crime prevention methods, we must treat extreme social deviance in a different way because the initial motives are not an indictment of society but a reaction against it.

A society which preaches and encourages individualism amongst its participants runs the risk of developing attitudes of extreme elitism and isolationism. Either of these in excess breeds insecurity and fear. Eventually the participants of any social system must accept that they need to be interdependent rather than self-reliant. Personal independence is a void concept unless it can be appreciated by others, and then it is no longer true independence. Only by developing a mutual dependence can individuals hope to attain the communal strength which is necessary to defeat an attacker who violates the individual and slowly destroys the society of which he forms a part.

If we are to succeed in the prevention of crime to a level which is acceptable by society, then it is vital that society plays its part.

The primary object of an efficient police force is the prevention of crime; the next is that of the detection and punishment of offenders if crime is committed. To these ends all efforts must be directed.

Since Sir Richard Mayne gave his job description of a police officer, the emphasis has shifted. It has become fashionable to quantify and evaluate every imaginable thing. What cannot be accurately quantified has become automatically suspect. Accordingly, the practice of crime prevention — the anticipation, recognition and appraisal of circumstances that increase the risk of crime and the initiation of action to reduce that risk — has become increasingly less fashionable.

A police service in Great Britain large enough to make any impression on crime by its physical presence would be economically prohibitive.

The explosion in the late seventies and early eighties of technology relating to the prevention of crime cannot be denied, together with the advent of satellite communication, yet crime still increases at an alarming rate.

In spite of modern technology, to succeed in terms of crime prevention, it would appear that the more traditional forms of community living must be re-introduced in order that a more caring and resonsible citizen can emerge. This will involve the changing of attitudes of government architects and planners, the high rise flats and tenement buildings must give way to smaller family units where individuals both juvenile and adult can obtain a sense of belonging and an identity of their own as opposed to one enforced upon them by authority incarcerating them into nothing more than concrete prisons.

The social consequences of long-term unemployment must be catered for in addition to the increase of leisure time ensuring that these are not reflected in higher crime rates. This is particularly important when related to the young. These needs must be provided for by the supplying of sporting and cultural facilities open to all irrespective of social or financial standing, and perhaps emphasis being placed on projects to provide adventure and challenge to the young.

The cost of providing the foregoing will be great, but can society or authority fail to afford the capital cost of supplying such facilities when one considers the alternative costs of increasing crime and vandalism, not taking into account the incalculable cost of a deterioration in the quality of life or peace of mind.

Throughout time *Cost Effective* crime prevention has been the key words. Traditionally in Great Britain all crime prevention initiatives have been financed from police budgets. It is only in the eighties that sponsorship for crime prevention projects has become fashionable. I have no doubt that this is a trend which must continue. National and multinational companies, together with smaller retailers and industrialists, must be prepared to support police initiatives. Crime Prevention Panels established in Great Britain in the early seventies must increase numerically throughout the land, and also in efficiency. These are organisations set up with Police Force areas of local citizens who liaise with and assist the police in the fight against crime.

The future of modern society rests with the young and no country will succeed in reducing crime without extensive educational programmes commencing in the primary schools, i.e. aged 6 years — 10 years, and continuing through the higher grades.

During this educational programme the young must achieve four objectives:

(a) Develop a greater awareness of social and personal consequences of criminal behaviour both for the offender and victim.

(b) Develop a greater insight into roles of the agencies involved with the legal system.

(c) Develop their understanding of the principles underlying the legal system by examining the rationale behind law making.

(d) Develop an understanding of the premises which exist within peer groups and how these premises can affect behaviour.

It is surprising that given Great Britain has been recognised as the country to give birth to the modern police force and, perhaps, more so given the direction of Sir Robert Mayne, that in 1984 it has become necessary for the government of Great Britain to re-emphasise the importance of crime prevention to society in the form of a circular under the signatures of five government departments, namely the Home Office, the Department of Education and Science, the Department of the Environment, the Welsh Office and the Department of Health and Social Security. The birth of a new century could herald the rebirth of crime prevention with what I consider to be the basis for crime prevention in the twenty-first century — a multi-agency approach to the prevention of crime. The prevention of crime is for anyone and everyone, unity is strength and it is only when all agencies and the community work together that a reduction in crime will result.

Experience indicates that a sound policy towards crime prevention should take into account the following points:

(a) effective crime prevention needs the active support of the community. The methods used by the police are constantly improving but police effectiveness cannot be greatly increased unless the community can be persuaded to do more for itself;

(b) crime prevention schemes are more successful where the police and local agencies work together in a co-ordinated way towards particular aims;

(c) patterns of crime vary greatly from one area to the next. Preventive measures are therefore more likely to be successful when designed to reflect local characteristics and focused on particular types of crime;

(d) whilst there is a need to address the social factors associated with criminal behaviour, and policies are continually being devised to tackle this aspect of the problem, these are essentially long-term measures. For the short term, the best way forward is to reduce through management, design or changes in the environment the opportunities that exist for crime to occur.

The public can only be expected to help in preventing crime where initiatives against it reflect their own perceptions and concerns; otherwise their involvement would almost certainly be minimal. This indicates a need for methods by which the community's fears and concerns can be assessed, and for the formation of closer links between the public and those holding positions of authority.

Prevention can form only one part of the strategy against crime. However, there is growing recognition within the police service and elsewhere of the scope for placing greater emphasis on preventive measures. This does not mean that progress in the prevention of crime will be achieved quickly or easily. Nonetheless, much useful activity is already under way; this must be built on to ensure that the potential that exists in the community to prevent crime is fully harnessed. A co-ordinated response is required at all levels: from members of the public, both as individuals and within agencies, and by agencies working together. If crime is to be reduced, prevention must be given the priority to deserves and must become a responsibility of the community as a whole.

10

Asset Protection — A Far Eastern Approach for the Future

Prof. Jose B. Maniwong

Dean, College of Criminology
Angeles University Foundation
and
President, Security & Safety
Corporation of the Philippines

Assets Protection

Assets, whether belonging to a person or a corporation, must necessarily be protected. Today, in the Far East as well as in any other part of the world, assets are protected by either the government, by private security or by both. Protection of life and property against criminal attacks is a governmental function. But, it is indeed a truism that the government alone cannot cope with the protection of assets. There is the necessity of the private sector to do its share in such protection.

This dissertation has for its theme the role of private security in asset protection now and in the future.

Today, industry operates in an environment highly susceptible to economic influences and fluctuations. Industry's viability is invariably buttressed in the state of the country's economy. The need for expanded private security comes with progress.

The clientele of the private security industry now demand a total spectrum of security services. Guard and patrol services, investigative and detective services, armored car and armed services, alarm systems, and many more are now demanded of the private security industry. This is brought about by the complexities of the efforts of elements disturbing peaceful possession of assets.

The private security industry's growth is propelled by population growth, industrial expansion, urbanization, countryside development, and government reforms. Because of these, the private security industry must have its own development in order that it may be more effective.

There will be an increasing demand for the private security industry's role in the protection of assets. But the industry has its own problems. The need for professionalization and the lack of solid financial resources to support the industry in its need for the technology hardware now available, the sub-standard quality of personnel, and the low level of financial commitment of the industry's clientele, are but few of the problems encountered by the industry.

The private security industry's presence in our contemporary life cannot, it would seem, be eliminated with the inability of the government to provide the needed protection for the people's assets. It is imperative therefore that security and protective services must respond with timeliness and efficiency to the demands of the private sector's welfare and public safety.

There is nothing permanent in this world except change and with such change many changes in many aspects of life also go. But is said that in order that we can understand the present, we must know the past, and understand the present we can more or less surmise what the future will be.

Asset protection at present is not as simple as it may appear. Every day changes happen. The need for better and adequate technology appears. What will then asset protection be in the future?

Thefts and Abuses — Against Computers[1]

Thefts and abuses involving computers have proven to be both daily and costly occurrences for the modern-day organization. Management would be ill-advised to dismiss them. For example:

- Dishonest corporate officials used a company's computer to create fictitious policies. Losses to the company's stockholders exceeded $1 billion.
- Bogus computer reports were used to defraud investors out of $40 million.
- Criminals used a railroad company's computers to divert 2,800 of its boxcars; only 250 were recovered. Losses to the company exceeded $100 million.
- A Fortune 500 company went bankrupt after it was discovered that dishonest officials had inflated its revenues with the aid of the company's computer. Losses to the stockholders exceeded $50 million.
- A computer was used to embezzle more that $20 million from a financial institution.
- Computer-connected crimes and abuses, like other forms of criminal conduct, fall into one or more categories. These often take the following forms:
  - Theft of data;
  - Diversion of property;
  - Unauthorized use;
  - Vandalism;
  - Financial frauds.

In an increasingly computerized business environment, information takes on a value of its own. In today's business world, trade secrets, programs, mailing lists, confidential marketing plans, and other valuable financial data have become valuable commodities. Competitors, and even foreign governments, are willing buyers; criminal prosecutions are the exception rather than the norm. The theft of data is now big business.

The ease with which computer-connected information crimes can be perpetrated was amply illustrated by several dishonest employees of a catalogue company; they copied their employer's most valued customer list and old it to a competitor. These informational crimes are especially common in business environments where programs and files are loosely controlled and also where system services and physical facilities are readily available to the public or to employees during non-working hours.

The diversion of valuable merchandise, goods or other property through the use of a computer, is a serious and growing problem for business. For example, criminals armed with the secret access code of a company's computer were able to telephone their orders and instruct the computer where to ship the merchandise. By the time the case finally surfaced, the victim had been taken for more than $1 million. In an increasingly automated retail environment, the use of computers as vehicles for property crimes is on the increase.

The unauthorized use of its computers poses a problem for every organization. It is not uncommon for an employee to use his employer's computer to play games or conduct personal business. Since computer time can prove costly, the unauthorized use of its computers can prove expensive to a company.

In one such case, a computer systems manager is said to have cost his employer more than $40,000 in computer time; the dishonest employee used the computer to store personal financial data. Prosecutions in this area are rare; courts are reluctant to convict under local theft of services statutes.[1]

What is Adequate Security

It is submitted that everyone must be concerned with the future because everybody will have to live with it. We have to be prepared for the protection of assets in the future. Enemies of society can attack anytime. Assets face that risk which is at most times unpredictable. The best way therefore to manage such a risk is to provide adequate security. But what is "adequate security?" How can it be provided when the kind of risk is unforeseeable? But it must be admitted that with certain kinds of information, companies can foresee the probability, or even a certain level of probability, that a crime will occur. . . Especially if such crime has already occurred in that company before.

Once a crime is deemed to be reasonably foreseeable, an even tougher question arises about what kind of security measures are reasonably adequate to prevent it. Many people have strong opinions about what works to prevent crime, but few (if any) scientific tests are available to serve as objective evidence. In the absence of such research, what is "adequate security" may be a matter of weighing a judge's opinion against a security manager's view on the same subject.

Feasibility of the Crime

On the issue of feasibility, what proper standard of prior history of attacks will suffice to make them foreseeable? Will it be the specific crime at each specific location? The location of a plant or company in a generally high crime neighborhood? Or where specific crimes have been known to occur?

When crimes or attacks against assets are foreseeable, adequate security can and must be provided. The issue of foreseeability, then, poses a number of questions security professionals can address. What is the proper standard of prior history of crimes that makes them foreseeable? Which one of the following standards should apply: each specific location; crimes of any sort at each specific location; the location of a facility in a generally high crime neighborhood; or the location of a facility in an area where a specific type of crime has been known to occur? How many crimes should be on record and how recently should they have occurred in order to make another crime foreseeable? How should a "high crime area" be defined — by geographic scope or by the rate of crimes per 100,000 inhabitants?

The courts now look for a "reasonable" answer to these questions, but once again different answers are rendered in different cases. Who is better suited to establish some clear standards about what is reasonable than security professionals?[2]

Private Security

Modern private security in the Far East did not just spring up during the last part of the 20th century fully formed as it is now. A perusal of private security in the Far East started from an individual hired to "open and close" the gate when the owner comes. Later more individuals were called upon to provide security. Then sprung the private security industry as we know it now.

Then came the public versus private policing. It became apparent that government functions is inadequate to protect life and property from criminal attacks. The change in property relations, the proliferation of plants and corporations, the shift from small toward large, corporate holdings, explains the growth of private security. With this growth of the industry came the need for security hardware and specialized expertise.

The demand for greater security in the Far East is growing. Fast expansion in industrialization and technology is taking place in this part of the world, thus security becomes more complex. Even the American Society for Industrial Security is growing in the Far East. In the next fifteen years, tremendous growth will be taking place in Japan, Australia and the Philippine Islands.

The enemies of society improve their technology as the government and the private sector improve their expertise to combat them. What then lies ahead? It is submitted that technologies and hardware for combatting crime will improve in the future. What is deemed efficient now may become obsolete in the future. The faculty of men is so creative that its capability for anything seems almost unlimited. Where asset protection in the future may be different from what is traditional now, what is to be done?

Progress & Motivation

By the years 2000 *progressive security managers* will realize that their job as managers of assets will be growing with wider responsibilities, plus an array of specialities, i.e. corporate investigators as well as operational investigators, physical security engineers, executive protection specialists, loss prevention specialists, fire prevention specialists, and computer security specialists — all reporting to the Director of Security or his Chief Security Officer. Plus, he must be able to motivate his employees.

How to Motivate Employees?

The psychology of motivation is tremendously complex and what has been unraveled with any degree of assurance is small indeed.

Motivation techniques will be the same in the year 2000 as they are now:

1. development of off-hour recreation programs;
2. spiraling wages;
3. fringe benefits;
4. human relations training;
5. sensitivity training;
6. communications;
7. two-way communication;
8. job participation;
9. employee counseling.

Factors affecting job attitudes are: security, status, relationship with subordinates, personal life, relationship with peers, salary, benefits, relationship with supervisor, supervision, growth, advancement, responsibility, recognition and achievement.

People cause crimes to occur and people and technology will have to be used to reduce or to prevent crimes from occurring.

To sell its services to the clientele, private security should:

1. Professionalize security services. Tom Peters, with Robert Waterman wrote the book, *In Search of Excellence."* Then with Nancy Austin, Tom Peters wrote *A Passion for Excellence.* These two books should be on every manager's bookshelf. The concepts discussed will make managers aware of professional services and the rewards received from providing such services.
2. Improvement of present security operational standards. Do we do it or do we wait for insurance companies to

set standards for operational disciplines and our perfor-mance?

3. Train personnel to properly operate the technological hardware of the industry and retrain them to handle improvements of such hardware. Training should be established to improve skills of upper management as well as lower staff members. Plus, education of our respective communities in matters related to security and personal safety.

4. Overall satellites will be playing an important part in future security programs and we should be ready to meet the challenge.

Robots

It is said, "If technology continues its boom at its current rate, in the year 2000 few people will be working as security guards. Perhaps by the year 1990, robotized computers will perform many of the security functions handled today by human hands and other less sophisticated security equipment. By that time, most contract guard agencies will have evolved into security robot firms."

If the above is to happen, it is imperative that the private security industry update its expertise on technical and mechanical matters as a preparation for the future when and if robotized computers perform some of the functions of the traditional security guard.

To cope with the future, the private security industry should:

1. Keep abreast with improved technologies, state of the art hardware and establish standards;
2. Improve its career development;
3. Keep on foreseeing the foreseeable future — life's com-plexities in the future and its challenges;
4. Keep updated statistics on crimes against assets in different localities, in different corporations and/or plants. These statistics will form the base for future projections on security.
5. In the Far East, private security should be governed and supervised by the government under a "Private

Security Authority Law." Some government in the Far East without such a law should endeavor to have one. Armed private security personnel should not be allowed to be supervised by private entities alone, rather should be in a close supervision and control by the government.

1. *Computers & Business # Liabilities: A Preventive Guide for Management* by August Bequai, Esp. Published by Washington Legal Foundation, 1984.
2. "What is Adequate Security," *Security Management,* Jan. 1983, Lawrence W. Sherman & Eva F. Sherman
3. Ibid

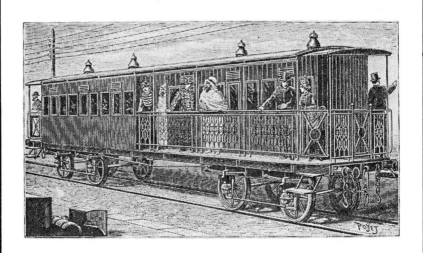

11

The Future Course of International Terrorism*

Brian Michael Jenkins

International terrorism emerged as a problem in the late 1960s and despite increased governmental efforts to combat it, terrorism remains a serious problem in the 1980s. Will terrorism continue? Yes.

Political violence in one form or another has existed for centuries. Earlier waves of terrorist violence at the beginning of the century and again in the 1920's and 1930's were eclipsed only by world wars.

Terrorist activity accompanied postwar decolonization, which continued up through the 1960's. Some of the colonial liberation movements, most notably the Algerian FLN, provided a model for later terrorists groups.

Modern theories of guerrilla way — which, of course, is not synonymous with terrorism but did contribute doctrinally to the use of terrorists tactics — developed during this same period, from the late 1940's to the early 1960's. World War II represented the culmination of state-organized violence.

---

*An earlier version of this paper was presented by the author of the International Conference on Current Trends in World Terrorism, Tel Aviv, Israel, July 1-4, 1985

Since then, there has been a long range trend toward the "privatization" of violence.

All of these facts argue for the continuation of some kind of political violence outside of conventional warfare, but will international terrorism persist in its present form? I think it will, for a number of reasons:

International terrorism as we know it today had its origins in the political circumstances that prevailed at the end of the 1960's: the frustration of the Palestinian Arabs after Israel's crushing defeat of the Arab armies in 1967; the failure of Latin America's guerrillas to duplicate the success of Castro's revolution in Cuba and their increasing attention to the struggle inthe cities, which led to the increasing use of terrorist tactics; the swas in Vietnam, which galvanized a generation of youth in America, Western Europe, and Japan to protest in the streets, and resulted in a few at the extremist fringe carrying on the protest with guns and bombs.

But, in contemporary international terrorism also reflected some recent technological developments which enhanced the use of terrorist tactics:

- Modern air travel provided unprecedented worldwide mobility.
- Radio, television, and communications satellites provided almost instantaneous access to a to a worldwide audience.
- Weapons and explosives became increasingly available to anybody with the money to buy them.
- Modern society offered new vulnerabilities, in particular, airplanes.

Political circumstances may change but these technological developments have permanently altered the environment.

The first generation of modern terrorists has provided a model of behavior. Terrorist have become a routine way of focusing attention on a dispute, of bringing pressure on a government. New causes and new groups have emerged — Armenian terrorists., Sikh terrorists, issue-oriented groups opposed to nuclear power, abortion, technology, pollution, animal vivisection. There certainly will be no lack of causes.

There are economic incentives to use terrorist tactics.

Kidnapping and extortion based upon threats of violence have become routine means of financing revolutionary movements.

A semi-permanent infrastructure of support has emerged. Beneath the terrorist groups, and supporting them often without regard to ideology or cause, is an ephemeral but resilient network of connections, alliances, safe houses, arms suppliers, and provisioners of counterfeit documents and other services. This network resembles the infrastructure that suports organized crime.

States have recognized in terrorism a useful weapon and are eploiting it for their own purposes. To a certain extent, international terrorism has become institutionalized.

And, increasingly, terrorism is expected and "tolerated."

All these reasons suggest that terrorism as we know it now is likely to persist as a mode of political expression for various groups, and as a means of warfare among states. It probably will continue, but at what level? *Will we see more or less terrorism?* Measured by the number of incidents,

terrorism has increased in volume over the last 17 years. It is a ragged increase, with peaks and valleys, but the overall trajectory In clearly upward. There were, for example, four times as many incidents of international terrorism in 1984 as there were in 1972, the year of the Munich attack. Insofar as we can tell, the increase in genuine — it is not due merely to better reporting. The increase in the late 1970s and the early 1980s was quite dramatic. Terrorist activity, according to our figures, leveled off in 1984, but based upon the figures from the first five months of this year, it looks as if 1985 will surpass all previous years in the volume of activity.

Overall, the annual growth rate in the volume of terrorist activity has been in the area of 12 to 15 percent. If that rate of increase continues, we could see something between 800 and 900 incidents a year by the end of the decade, which is not inconceivable given the other factors I have mentioned.

There are several other factors which suggest the likelihood of continued growth:
1. The increase in the volume of terrorist activity has been matched by its geographic spread — a slow, long-term

trend. The number of countries experiencing some sort of terrorist activity each year has gradually increased.

2. Although a handful of nations — the United States, France, Israel, the United Kingdom, and Turkey::remain the favorite targets of terrorists and account for approximately half of all the victims, the number of nations targeted by terrorists has also increased. Last year we saw terrorist attacks directed against the nationals of 60 countries.

3. Although it is difficult to monitor with any precision the appearance and disappearance of the many hundreds of groups that claim credit for terrorist actions — some of them are only fictitious banners — the level of international terrorist activity no longer appears to depend on a handful of groups. Despite the virtual destruction of some terrorist groups and the decline in operations by others, the total volume of terrorist activity grows.

4. As international communications spread, as populations move or are pushed about — two features of the 1980s — I suspect we may see more local conflicts manifesting themselves at the international level through terrorist tactics.

Will terrorists escalate? Simply killing a lot of people has seldom been a terrorist objective. As I have said on numerous occasions, terrorists want a lot of people *watching,* not a lot of people *dead.* Terrorists operate on the principle of the minimum force necessary. They find it unnecessary to kill many, as long as killing a few suffices for their for their purposes.

Statistics bear this out. Only 15 to 20 percent of all terrorist incidents involve fatalities; and of those, two-thirds involve only one death. Less than 1 percent of the thousands of terrorist incidents that have occurred in the last two decades involve 10 or more fatalities, and incidents of mass murder are truly rare.

Arbitrarily taking 100 deaths as the criterion, only a handful of incidents of this scale have occurred since the beginning of the century. Lowering the criterion to 50 deaths produces a dozen or more additional incidents. To get even a meaningful sample, the criterion has to be lowered to 25. This in itself suggests that it is either very hard to kill large numbers of persons, or it is very rarely tried.

Unfortunately, as we have seen in recent years, things are changing. Terrorist activity over the last 20 years has escalated in volume and in bloodshed. At the beginning of the 1970s, terrorists concentrated their attacks on property. In the 1980s, according to U.S. government statistics, half of all terrorist attacks have been directed against people. The number of incidents with fatalities and multiple fatalities has increased. A more alarming trend in the 1980s has been the growing number of incidents of large-scale indiscriminate violence: huge car bombs detonated on city streets, bombs planted aboard trains and airliners, in airline terminals, railroad stations, and hotel lobbies, all calculated to kill in quantity. Ten major international terrorist incidents have resulted in a total of more than 1000 deaths in the last 15 years, but more than two:thirds of these have occurred in the last two years.

There are several explanations for the escalation:

1. Like soldiers in a war, terrorists who have been in the field for many years have been brutalized by the long struggle; killing becomes easier.

2. As terrorism has become more commonplace, the public has become to a degree desensitized. Terrorists can no longer obtain the same amount of publicity using the same tactics they used 10 years ago, and they may feel compelled to escalate their violence inorder to keep public attention or to recover coercive power lost as governments have become more resistant to their demands.

3. Terrorists have become technically more proficient, enabling them to operate on a higher level of violence.

4. The composition of some terrorist groups has changed as the faint-hearted who have no stomach for indiscriminate killing drop out or are shoved aside by more ruthless elements.

5. The religious aspect of current conflicts in the Middle East pushes toward mass murder. As we have seen throughout history, the presumed approval of God for the killing of pagans, heathens, or infidels can permit acts of great destruction and self-destruction.

6. And finally, state sponsorship has provided terrorists with

the resources and technical know-how to operate at a higher, more lethal level of violence.

At the same time, severl factors work against escalation: There are self-imposed constraints, which I will address later, and there are technical ceilings. Without resorting to more exotic weapons, terrorists are approaching limits to their violence. The deadliest terrorist incidents — huge bombs detonated in buildings, the bomb presumably detonated aboard the Air India jumbo jet, a deliberately set fire in a crowded Teheran theater — each of which produced several hundred deaths, roughly equal the worst accidental disasters: hotel fires,, explosions, airline crashes. Death on a larger scale is seen only in the slaughter of great battles or in natural disasters like earthquakes and floods. The most plausible scenarios involving chemical or biological weapons in a contained environment — a hotel, a convention, a banquet — would produce deaths in the hundreds. To get above that, terrorists would have to possess large quantities of deadly substances and solve problems of dispersal, or they would have to resort to nuclear weapons. But this raises questions of technical capacity and intentions, which I will deal with momentarily.

A third limiting factor is security. Protective measures taken in the wake of the huge car and truck bombings in the Middle East are reducing the vulnerability of the most obvious targets to this type of attack. More stringent security measures may be applied on a permanent basis to prevent a repeat of the Air India bombing. Of course, terrorists can obviate these by shifting their sights to other, still vulnerable targets, but security measures force them to become even less discriminate.

On balance, it appears that incidents involving significant fatalities probably will become more common, with incidents resulting in hundreds of deaths remaining for the foreseeable future the outer limit of terrorists violence.

What changes will we see in terrorist tactics? I don't think we will see much tactical innovation. Terrorists operate with a fairly limited repertoire. Six basic tactics have accounted for 95 percent of all terrorist incidents; bombings, assassinations, armed assaults, kidnappings, hijackings, and barricade and hostage incidents. Looking at it another way, terrorists blow up things, kill people, or seize hostages. Every terrorist incident is merely a variation on these three activities.

There have been few changes in tactics over the years. Indeed, the relative percentage of the various tactics has remained stable for a number of years, except for a decline in barricade and hostage incidents. Seizing embassies was a popular tactic in the 1970s. It declined as security measures made embassy takeovers more difficult, and as governments became more resistant to the demands of terrorists holding hostages and more willing to use force to end such episodes, thus increasing the hostage-takers' risk of death or capture.

This is indicative of the kind of innovation we are likely to see. Terrorists innovate in an incremental way to solve specific problems created by security measures. If one tactic ceases to work, they abandon it in favor of another one or merely shift their sights to another target. Since terrorists have virtually unlimited targets, they have little need for tactical innovation.

For example, how might terrorists respond to the new security measures aimed at protecting embassies against can bombs? Conceivably, they might resort to aerial suicide attacks, which are technically and physically more demanding. Or they might resort to standoff attacks, the traditional response to strong defenses. Or they might simply detonate large bombs at other, still vulnerable targets. This brings me to the next question.

What changes will we see in terrorist targets? The greatest advantage that terrorists have and will continue to have is a virtually unlimited range of targets. Terrorists can attack anything, anywhere, anytime, limited only by operational considerations: Terrorists do not attack defended targets; they seek soft targets. If one target or set of targets is well protected, terrorists merely shift their sights to other targets that are not so well protected.

Over the years, the range of targets attacked by terrorists has expanded enormously. They now include embassies, airlines, airline terminals, ticket offices, trains, railroad stations, subways, buses, power lines, electrical transformers, mailboxes, mosques, hotels, restaurants, schools, libraries, churches, temples, newspapers, journalists, diplomats, businessmen, military officials, missionaries, priests, nuns, the Pope, men women, adults and children.

There are a few things terrorists have not done. With the exception of a couple of minor episodes, they have not attacked nuclear reactors. For the most part, terrorists have not operated at sea. There have been no attempts to take over offshore platforms. Prior to the recent hijack of the *Achille Lauro,* there had been a number of bombs planted aboard ships or mines planted on their hulls. There had been several ship hijackings and attempted hijackings suggesting that the idea of taking over a large vessel had crossed the terrorists' mind. Whether the recent hijackings will inspire imitation or other actions in the maritime environment remains to be seen. Terrorists have blown up computers and set fires in data processing centers, but they have not tried to penetrate computers in any sophisticated fashion to disrupt or destroy data.

What will be the future targets of terrorism? Pretty much the same ones they prefer today:

- Representatives of governments and symbols of nations — notable, diplomats and airlines.
- Representatives of economic systems — corporations and corporate executives.
- Symbols of policies and presence — military officials.
- Political leaders (in the past 15 years, terrorists have killed, tried to kill, or have been reported on their way to kill Carrero Blanco, Aldo More, Lord Mountbatten, Anwar Sadar, the Pope, Ronald Reagon, Indira Gandhhi, and Margaret Thatcher).

Will terrorists attack high-technology targets such as re- fineries, offshore platforms, or nuclear reactors? They already have, although in technically undemanding ways. Terrorists have blown up pylons and transformers, sometimes causing widespread blackouts. Guerrillas in Latin America have fre- quently attacked electrical power grids as a means of waging economic warfare, urban terrorists have attacked electrical energy systems to get attention, to protest government or corporate policies, or to indirectly disable nuclear power plants. Terrorist saboteurs have also attacked pipelines, oil tank farms, and refineries, again with the objective of attracting publicity or protesting specific policies. These targets will remain attractive to some groups. However, apparently not all terrorists see value in attacking energy systems. There is no discernible trend toward more frequent attacks. Moreover, to seriously disrupt energy systems requires either a sustained campaign or larger-scale action at certain critical nodes. Targets such as nuclear reactors or offshore platforms are technically demanding and require certain knowledge and skills.

Overall, attacks on high-technology targets must be anticipated as a feature of guerrilla warfare, but they are likely to remain only an occasional event in the realm of terrorism. State sponsorship, however, may alter targeting preferences.

Will we see a more sophisticated "white collar" terrorism, that is, attacks on telecommunications, data processing systems, or other targets where the terrorists' objective is not crude destruction but widespread disruption? Disruptive "terrorism" of this type may be more appealing to armchair terrorists than to those who are active in today's terrorist groups. We may occasionally see terrorist incidents of this type, but probably not many. Such operations are technically demanding, and they produce *no immediate visible effects.* There is no drama. No lives hang in the balance. There is no bang, no blood. They do not satisfy the hostility of the terrorists.

What weapons will terrorists use in the future? Terrorists now use what is readily available in the gunshops and arsenals or on the black market. They seek powerful, rapid-fire, concealable weapons. They use commercial explosives, military stuff when they can get it. These suffice for current operations. Since terrorists generally do not attack defended targets, they have no need for more advanced arms. They now match the firepower of the authorities. They have no need for sophisticated weapons. Terrorists probably will use more sophisticated explosives, in larger quantities, although there is no great need to increase quantity. Terrorists in the Middle

East have on several occasions built bombs containing more than a thousand pounds of explosives. Car bombs with 200 or more pounds of explosives are not uncommon. Fifteen to 20 pounds of Frangex planted inside a large building wil take off.

We will probably see increased use of standoff weapons-mortars, rocket launchers, rocket propelled grenades-to overcome security measures. Finally, there remains a potential for the use of portable precision-guided munitions, which terrorists already have employed on several occasions.

Will terrorists resort to weapons of mass destruction? Will they employ chemical or biological warfare? Will terrorists go nuclear? Many people believe that nuclear terrorism of some sort is likely and may be inevitable. Reflecting the results of a poll conducted among 1,346 opinion leaders in the United States, George Gallup Jr., in his recent book, Forecast 2000, wrote that "while a war between the superpowers, the U.S. and the Soviet Union, is a real cause for concern, (a disastrous nuclear incident involving terrorists in this country) seems to be the imminent danger."

I happen to think nuclear terrorism is neither imminent nor inevitable-if by nuclear terrorism we mean terrorists employing stolen nuclear weapons or a clandestinely fabricated nuclear explosive device to kill or threaten to kill large numbers of people. Lesser terrorist acts in the domain are possible-the seizure or attempted sabotage-of a nuclear reactor, the dispersal of radioactive material, an alarming nuclear hoax that may cause panic.

The question of nuclear terrorism involves an assessment of both capabilities and motivations. It is conceivable that someone outside of government who is familiar with the principles of nuclear weapons could design an atomic bomb. However, the ease with which someone outside of government can build one, assuming he or she had somehow acquired the necessary nuclear material, has been greatly exaggerated. But let's for a moment say they can. Would they want to? Terrorism has certainly escalated, but it is still a quantum jump from the kinds of things that terrorists do today to the realms of nuclear destruction. Why would terrorists take that jump?

As I said before, simply killing a lot of people is not an objective of terrorism. Terrorists could do more now, yet they don't. Why? Beyond the technical constraints, there may be self-imposed constraints that derive from moral considerations or political calculations. Some terrorists may view indiscriminate violence as immoral. The terrorists' enemy is the government, not the people. Also, terrorists pretend to be governments, and wanton murder might imperil the image.

There are political considerations as well: Terrorists fear alienating their perceived constitutents. They fear provoking public revulsion. They fear unleashing government crackdowns that their groups might not survive. Certainly, in the face of a nuclear threat, the rules that now limit police authorities in most democracies would change.

Terrorists must maintain group cohesion. Attitudes toward violence vary not only from group to group but also within a group. Inevitably, there would be disagreements over mass murder, which could expose the operation and the group to betrayal.

Obviously not all groups share the same operation code, and as we have seen, certain conditions or circumstances might erode these self-imposed constraints.

What about chemical or biological weapons, which are technically less demanding? Although there have been isolated incidents, neither chemical or biological warfare seems to fit the pattern of most terrorists attacks. These attacks are generally intended to produce immediate dramatic effects.

Terrorist incidents have a finite quality-an assassination, a bombing, a handful of deaths, and that is the end of the episode.

Finally, the terrorists retain control. That is quite different from initiating an event that offers no explosion but instead produces indiscriminate deaths and lingering illness, an event over which the terrorists who set it in motion would have little control. For the near-term future-say, the next five years-we are more likely to see threats of chemical or biological contamination made by authentic lunatics or criminal extortionists. There will be moments of alarm. Over the long-term-the next 10 to 15 years-my concern is that chemical weaponry will be acquired by unstable, dangerous countries like Iraq, Iran, or Syria, and will increasingly be used in warfare. If chemical warfare becomes more commonplace, particularly in a region like the Middle East, we cannot dismiss its potential use by terrorists. The same is true of nuclear weapons, but probably over a longer time period.

Where will terrorism fit in the future of armed conflict? I think the current trend toward state sponsor of terrorism will continue. As I have said before, limited conventional war, classic rural guerrilla, and international terrorism will coexist and may appear simultaneously. The Iranian revolution and its spread to Lebanon, which has involved the effective use of international terrorism as an instrument of policy, may provide a model for other Third World revolutions and revolutionary states, just as the Cuban model inspired a generation of imitators in Latin America. If it does, we are in for a lot of trouble.

- We also may see international terrorism emerge as a new kind of global guerrilla warfare in which terrorist groups sally forth from the political jungles of the Third World to carry out highly publicized hit-and-run attacks, militarily insignificant but politically of great consequence, avoiding confrontations where they might run into well-equipped, well-trained, specialized anti-terrorist forces.

Terrorists now avoid seizing embassies in Western capitals. They hijack airliners, keep them on the move to evade any rescue attempt, and retreat with their hostages to sanctuaries like Teheran or Beirut. Benefiting from the absence of government, as in Lebanon, or the presence of a hostile government, as in Iran, these sanctuaries lie beyond the reach of the world regime of treaty and law. If Iran defeats Iraq and the Gulf States fall, then the world's "badlands" might be centered in the Middle Est, a crescent reachng from the Mediterranean to Persia.

Finally, what developments will we see in security? We will see an increased diversion of resources to internal security.

- The "privatization" of violence has been matched by the "privatization" of security, as illustrated by the tremendous growth of private sector security expenditures. In the United States, a total of $21 billion is now spent annually for security services and hardware (as compared with $14 billion spent annually on all police). The figure will reach $50 to $60 billion a year by the end of the century. Private security corporations will grow to meet the demand.

We will see the further proliferation of inner perimeters, the rings of security that now surround airline terminals, government buildings, and, increasingly, corporate offices. from this last development, however, emerges a crude counter-terrorist strategy. by protecting the most obvious symbols, terrorists' preferred targets, terrorists will be forced to become less discriminate in their attacks. That will create greater public outrage, which governments can exploit to obtain domestic support and international cooperation to crush the terrorists.

In sum:

- Terrorism certainly will persist.
- Probably it will increase.
- Large-scale incidents will become more common.
- At the same time, I don't think terrorism will enter the mind-boggling world of high technology or mass destruction.
- In term of tactics, and weapons, terrorism will be for the foreseeable future a continuation of the past.
- States will continue to exploit terrorism-to use it for their own purposes. We may enter a protracted worldwide guerrilla war.
- And terrorists will create crises, forcing governments and corporations to divert more and more resources toward combatting them.

12

Terrorism and Beyond

The Rand Corporation

In the fall of 1980, 140 persons participated in an international conference on terrorism. The meeting, which was sponsored by several U.S. government agencies and hosted by The Rand Corporation in Santa Monica, California, brought together government officials and experts on terrorism from 13 countries to discuss various aspects of terrorism and low-level conflict and look to the future of political violence. Not surprisingly, the experts as a group tended to be cautious in their collective forecasts.

"Terrorism will remain a problem," the conference participants concluded. "There will be no shortage of sources of terrorism-increased poverty and scarcity; inflation and unemployment; increased tension between the have and have-not nations; waves of refugees and immigrants moving from poorer states to wealthier ones, often bringing with them the conflicts of their home country, sometimes causing resentment among native citizens; the disintegration of traditional authority structures; an increase in singe-issue groups; contentious issues such as nuclear power; the rise of aggressive fundamentalist religious groups or cults."

At the same time, however, not all participants were certain that these problems would lead automatically to terrorist violence. In his remarks, Ambassador Anthony C. E. Quainton, the director of the U.S. State Department's Office for Combatting Terrorism, noted that "It is widely assumed that racial tension, inflation, dwindling natural resources, rising population, and widening income disparities between and within countries will lead to higher levels of social frustration and violence. Some of this violence is presumed to be terroristic. Yet evidence of a connection between socioeconomic conditions and terrorism is inconclusive at best." Brian Jenkins also urged caution in jumping to conclusions in his introduction, pointing out that, "Thus far, research has not been able to demonstrate a connection between poverty, scarcity, or inflation and terrorism. Indeed, it is not demonstrable that poverty, scarcity, or inflation have actually increased over any defined period. Social observers frequently assert that traditional authority structures are collapsing or have collapsed. But they have said so for decades-during the industrial revolution, after the abolition of slavery, after World War I, after female suffrage, after World War II. Traditional authority structures are collapsing all the time. And are there more aggressive fundamentalist religious groups in the last quarter of the twentieth century than there were in the nineteenth century?"

There was consensus that "state support of terrorism through the provision of money, weapons, training, and asylum can be expected to continue, and it may increase." The participants also noted "an alarming trend toward the use of terrorism directly by states . . . usually against dissident nationals residing in a host country." Ambassador Quainton noted the consequences of this in his remarks: "There states, by their willingness to underwrite violence and subnational conflict, in fact create an atmosphere in which terrorism flourishes."

That raises a crucial conceptual question. "Is terrorism a well-defined list of criminal acts that are uniquely heinous because they are against "innocent" targets, or is it but one strategy in a continuum of low-level political violence no more or less reprehensible than insurgency or guerrilla warfare?

The United States has adopted the former approach. Consequently, we have focused our efforts on a series of deterrent and preventive measures and on a strengthening of international law to outlaw these acts. However, if governments accept the latter view, they will have to put counterterrorism into a foreign policy context in which their attitude toward violence will be conditioned by their attitude toward the cause on behalf of which violence is being used. The perils of this approach are manifest. Ends and means will be confused. Obviously many governments are torn between these approaches. They wish to have their cake and eat it too.

Conference participants devoted considerable attention to the question of escalation. Just how far would terrorists go? The participants identified several kinds of escalation. Individual acts of actual or potential catastrophic destruction-the use by terrorists of chemical, biological, or even nuclear weapons-are what most people have in mind when they discuss escalation. But there is also escalation in the choice of targets-for example, targeting energy grids, power stations, communications systems-with terrorists seeking greater disruption, not casualties. Either type of escalation could entail more sophisticated weapons without entering the domain of theoretical mass destruction." Or "terrorism might escalate in sheer volume without new weapons or new targets, threatening the fabric of society, or evolving into civil war." However, when the participants talked about escalation, they generally had in mind the first type.

They considered "two basic types of groups: (1) terrorists who are extremely conscious of public opinion and who worry about the effects of their acts, and (2) terrorists who are so convinced that their cause is righteous, claiming the sanction of God or subscribing to ideologies that denigrate the importance of favorable public opinion, that they may contemplate actions with no concern for casualties." This would include the Shi'ite extremist groups that have carried out many of the most murderous attacks during the last several years. It was felt that "we should be on the alert for an increase in groups of the latter sort, as they are the most likely to be extremely destructive and heedless of casualties." However, even groups that worry about the attitudes of their perceived constituency or about public opinion in general are seldom able to fine-tune their actions, and over time they tend to become more brutal, less mindful of constraints. Terrorist groups of the first type may with time become groups of the second type.

Most of the participants seemed to be "cautiously" optimistic about thermonuclear terrorism, thinking it was not likely to occur in the near future for a variety of reasons. First, the terrorists may feel the use of nuclear devices or a dangerous attack on installations could alienate real and imagined sympathizers. Second, terrorist groups seem determined to remain small, not just for security reasons but for reasons of cohesion, and therefore are not likely to aim for acquisition of super-capabilities. Finally, except for psychotics, most individuals, including terrorists, are not seen as eager to use superviolence against other people. One discussant called this a "corrective mechanism" at work in terrorist groups, keeping them from getting too violent, not only for fear of alienating constituents and bringing down upon themselves the wrath of the state and society, but also to avoid alienating their own members and to remain in a position to recruit new ones.

The question was raised as to who would be the most dangerous type of terrorist. It was agreed that the most dangerous terrorist would have to be an individual or group with a particularly pronounced tendency to despise human life and to regard opponents as non-people or mere objects. A group with this inclination would be likely to be of the millenialist type-perhaps a fanatical religious cult. Alternatively, it might be a group trying to escalate from mere terrorist activity and low-level or subnational conflict to the starting of war, possibly on behalf of some nation that would give them support.

Who will be the targets of terrorism in the future? Basically, the participants concluded, those who terrorists perceive as powerful. Energy companies, because of their increasing importance in the world economy, are the powerholders of the future. Those who control vast economic resources, such as multinational corporations. It was suggested that the projected energy crisis coupled with the increasing gap between the "have" and "have not" nations may influence future terrorism. Literature has already appeared urging that terrorism be used as one of the few levers left to some Third World countries. One participant even suggested that oil-producing states might use terrorism to prevent energy alternatives from being produced. Energy-related targets - including offshore drilling platforms, oil tankers, and offshore loading and transfer facilities - will be increasingly attractive to terrorists in the future. A corollary of this trend is that multinational interests will become more frequent targets, and therefore business and government will have to increasingly coordinate efforts to assess vulnerability, to provide protection, and to present a credible response to the terrorist threat.

Given such forecasts, the conference participants concluded that the cost of security and protection can only go up. As terrorists proliferate in number, as their targets widen, as they become technologically more adept, the difficulty of physically preventing terrorism will intensify.

TVI Survey Results

Major war with the Soviet Union is not very likely between now and the year 2000 but terrorism certainly will escalate. Terrorist attacks will occur in the United States and the United States will respond with military force. Apart from government targets, terrorists will direct their violence against public utilities, the oil and chemical industry, transportation, banks, industry, and tourism.

Those are the conclusions of law enforcement and military officials, diplomats, directors of corporate security, researchers and scholars worldwide - experts on terrorism and those on the front line in the many terrorist wars - the readers of TVI REPORT.

The overwhelming majority of TVI readers believe that terrorists will threaten greater violence in the future. Asked to "select which statement most closely reflects your view of the course of terrorism over the next twenty years," 48 percent thought that "by the year 2000, terrorists will employ chemical, biological, or nuclear weapons." Forty-four percent thought that "without changing their basic tactics, terrorists will continue to escalate their violence." Less than 7 percent thought that "we will see more of the same with no great change in terrorist tactics or targets, or in the level of terrorist violence." Hardly any of the respondents thought "terrorism will gradually diminish as a worldwide problem."

Asked to be more specific about the methods terrorists will use in the future, 55 percent thought it "very likely" that by the year 2000, terrorists would employ shoulder-fired, precision-guided surface-to-air missiles to shoot down civilian planes;" another 29 percent thought it somewhat likely. Thirty-nine percent thought it very likely that terrorists would penetrate computers to cause major disruption to government or corporation operators. Twenty-eight percent thought it "very likely" and another 43 percent thought it "somewhat likely" that terrorists would conduct routine operations in the maritime environment attacking ships at sea or off-shore platforms. (While results of this poll were being received, terrorists seized the Italian luxury liner *Achille Lauro*.) Most readers, more than 85 percent, thought it "very likely" and another 37 percent though it "somewhat likely" that terrorists would attack energy systems and power grids to cause widespread blackouts. Respondents were less certain that terrorists would try to seize nuclear facilities: 23 percent thought it "very likely;" 48 percent thought it "somewhat likely," and 28 percent considered it "not very likely."

Although the majority of the respondents in answering Question Number 1 thought that by the year 2000 terrorists would employ chemical, biological, or nuclear weapons, they were somewhat doubtful when the question specified nuclear weapons: 28 percent thought it "somewhat likely" while 47 percent thought it "not very likely." At the opposite ends of the spectrum, 11 percent thought it "very likely" while 15 percent considered it "not at all likely."

They were more certain, when the question specified the employment of "chemical or biological weapons in such a way as to cause or threaten widespread casualties": 30 percent considered it "very likely;" 39 percent considered it "somewhat likely;" while 27 percent considered it "not very likely."

As to the most likely sources of future terrorist violence, "state-sponsorship," "ethnic conflict and separatist struggles," and "religious fanaticism" were the three most frequently selected, followed closely by "ideological conflict" and distantly by "contentious issues such as abortion, animal vivisection and environmental pollution." Responses to the next question confirmed the view that TVI readers believe state-sponsored terrorism to be the major problem of the future. Asked whether they thought state-sponsored terrorism would increase or decrease during the next 20 years, by a margin of more than 10 to 1, respondents thought it would increase.

Given their certainty that state-sponsored terrorism would increase particularly against Americans abroad, who already are the number one targets in international terrorism, most respondents - 70 percent - believed that the United States would respond with military force against terrorists or their state sponsors within the next five years. It is interesting to note here, however, that nearly a quarter of those surveyed were "doubtful that the United States will ever respond with military force."

More than 70 percent of the respondents expected to see "major terrorist attacks launched or instigated from abroad to occur in the United States within the next five years. Another 22 percent thought they certainly would occur by the year 2000.

What about the future shape of conflict? Asked how the United States armed forces were most likely to be employed between now and the year 2000, 53 percent thought it "not very likely" and another 36 percent found it "not at all likely" that the United States would be involved in a major war with the Soviet Union. Opinion divided more evenly on the prospects of the U.S. involvement in a limited conventional war: 49 percent thought it "somewhat likely" while 32 percent found it "not very likely." Respondents thought it much more likely that the United States would be involved in providing assistance to a Third World ally engaged in fighting or insurgency: 61 percent thought it "very likely," another 37 percent thought it "somewhat likely." Respondents also found it more probable that the United States armed forces would be engaged in responding to terrorists either in the rescue of hostages or reprisal operations: 71 percent considered it "very likely;" another 17 percent thought it "somewhat likely."

As for the most likely commercial targets of terrorism in the future, basic utilities and communications systems and oil and chemical facilities led the list. More than 90 percent of the respondents identified utilities (gas, electric, nuclear, water systems) and communications as a likely target while 79 percent selected oil and chemical facilities. These were followed by the transportation industry with 78 percent, financial institutions with 72 percent, industrial targets with 60 percent, and tourism, hotel and recreational facilities with 53 percent.

We asked respondents what, in their opinion, was the most significant terrorist threat of the future. State-sponsored terrorism clearly worried most people. American readers were concerned that state-sponsored terrorist groups, perhaps working with local confederates, would carry out attacked in the United States; this ranked fourth on the list of threats. Acquisition by terrorists of chemical or biological weapons ranked second among the potential threats. Acquisition by terrorists of chemical or biological weapons ranked second among the potential threats. Nuclear blackmail by terrorists ranked third. Not surprisingly given recent headlines, suicide bombers and other religiously inspired fanatics also caused great consternation among our respondents. Other candidates for the most significant terrorist threat included the possibility that terrorists armed with sophisticated new weapons will shoot down civilian aircraft or carry out other attacks causing large-scale casualties. One reader pointed to the possibility of growing political turmoil in Central America and Mexico which could put terrorism on the United States' southern border. Others warned that the grested threat comes not from the terrorist themselves, but rather from the consequences of overreaction to terrorism - blind military retaliation, the reduction of personal freedoms in an atmosphere of alarm.

We also asked respondents to identify what they thought

would be the most significant type of criminal activity in the future. Computer crime led the list. In the opinion of TVI's readers, criminals will continue to penetrate computers for the purpose of theft. The respondents also worried that terrorists, for a variety of motives, would try to destroy or sabotage computerized data bases or penetrate computers, causing various forms of political, economic, and social disruption. They considered drugs to be the second most important problem. Respondents seemed less concerned with individual drug use than with the violent crime that is associated with drug use and drug smuggling. A close third among the significant types of criminal activity was the growing problem of extortion based upon the contamination or threatened contamination of food, pharmaceutical products, or water supplies. This seems to have become an increasingly fashionable, if often unreported, crime in the 1980's.

Personal-injury extortion also seems to be increasing and was mentioned as a significant problem. Many of the U.S. respondents also worried that ransom kidnapping, a comparatively rare crime in the United States, would come to this country.

White-collar crime other than computer crime was also mentioned as the crime of the future. Some respondents pointed to growing violent crime or less focused urban violence as the greater threat to society. A number of the respondents mentioned the related problems of industrial espionage, technology theft, and illegal trafficking in high-tech commodities, including weapons. One respondent worried about the development of a black market for chemical, biological, or nuclear materials suitable for use in weapons.

Other respondents feared the emergence of new connections among drug traffickers, organized crime, terrorists, and guerrillas that could create a powerful alliance between the underworld and the underground.

Recalling recent bank scandals, one respondent thought the most significant crimes of the future might come from financial manipulation of or by financial institutions. Several others thought assassinations by political extremists or criminals seeking revenge against government officials would pose a major criminal threat. Finally, one expressed concern that criminals might find some way to exploit developments in the field of genetic engineering to create as yet unimaginable crimes.

13

Women in Security in the Year 2000

Darlene Sherwood, CPP

Manager, Security Administrative Services

SRI International, Menlo Park, CA

"At this point in our history it takes a very special type of woman to succeed in one of the male-dominated professions because the pressures on her from all sides are so very great."[1]
THEODORE S. KISSEL

Today more women are entering the security field and being promoted to supervisory and management positions more frequently than at any other time in our history. They are taking a more active part in security professional societies and are attending more security seminars, workshops, and formal educational courses.

Women find the security field to be challenging, growing, changing and important to industry and government, so they will continue to be attracted to the profession.

Almost all of the women that I know who are currently in security management positions began their careers in secretarial, clerical or administrative assistant positions within a security department. They were promoted to supervisory or management positions with their companies, and have either remained in management positions with those companies or transferred to other companies in similar capacities. A number of women have entered the security field upon leaving the military.

On-the-job experience in security is extremely valuable, but advanced education and training are necessary for women who expect to compete for senior management positions.

It took almost 200 years to gain equality in education, but women have begun to reap the rewards of attending institutions of higher learning. According to the Bureau of the Census, more women than men are currently attending colleges and universities in every major geographical area of the United States except the Mountain States (Montana, Idaho, Wyoming, Colorado, New Mexico, Arizona, Utah, and Nevada).[2]

It is predicted that as more women complete college, they will enter the professions. In the future, more educational courses will be offered through computers, video cassettes, and television. More specialized educational facilities will be available to meet the needs of full time employees and those needing child care in order to attend classes.

Professional workers such as teachers, engineers, lawyers, computer programmers, doctors, nurses, social workers, accountants, and librarians already make up 11 percent of the work force, half of which are women. These professionals and the security professionals alike are information workers. John Naisbett, *Megatrends,* says that for the professional, "the creation, processing, and distribution of information *is* the job."[3] More women will be attracted to the security profession as information workers.

"A new group can come into being only when the culture is receptive to new symbols of identity," says Jeane J. Kirkpatrick.[4] We are still working on reform, and it was only on July 20, 1968, that the Fourteenth Amendment added women's right to due process of law and equal protection of the laws.[5] Today women have a greater voice in their own role in the labor market, and they will be elected and given government appointments, so reform will continue.

Resistance toward women taking over senior management jobs still exists, but with advanced education and experience, they are able to handle the decisions required and the challenges of managing organizations. Intelligence, timing, patience, business and social skills will continue to contribute to the success of women managers and executives of the future.

The security profession is undergoing a significant transition period with more women competing for security management positions where as this was practically nonexistent in the past. Such transition requires a high degree of tolerance, but generally, if men perceive that a woman does her homework, makes tough decisions, solves problems, and works effectively with others, there is a more positive acceptance of her is the management structure.

Reform will continue, but laws and regulations change much faster than attitudes. It was socially acceptable for so long to be biased towards women in male-dominated fields that some men believe that their thinking or feelings are justified. Many are making a concerted effort to overcome their prejudicial thinking toward women, and others are geniunely supportive and encouraging to women in security.

THE 1980S

"The single most oustanding phenomenon of the century is the flood of women into jobs," said Eli Ginzberg.[6] In 1950, 34 percent of all U.S. women were part of the labor force. In 1980 the percentage grew to 51 percent, and 75 percent of American women are expected to be in the work force by 1990.[7]

In 1983, 53 percent of the women were working with married women making up the largest component, 55.7 percent.[8] This will continue to have a profound effect of life styles, relationships, real estate, politics, and government.[9]

The married working woman is the newest member of the labor force. At the beginning of the 1980s, in 31 percent of U.S. families both husband and wife worked. By 1990 it is projected that 40 percent of U.S. households will have two incomes, representing more than half of the U.S. consumer income.[10]

Two thirds of the growth in the labor force in the 80s and 90s will result from working women in the 20-44 age group. Overall growth in the next ten years will be influenced by the baby-boom generation (born between 1946 and 1964), but the uncertainties of regulations, prices, and unemployment will affect the growth projections.[11]

The growth of women in the work force has been largely based on: 1) increased opportunity, 2) economic reasons such as buying a home, rising expectations of standard of living, and an inflationary economy, 3) higher levels of education, 4) increased work experience, 5) professional aspirations, 6) demand for women in jobs formally held only by men, 7) social values changing where men do not feel inadequate if their wives work, 8) new jobs available through economic growth, computer-related jobs, health care jobs, 9) technology to help with chores and prepare meals faster.[12]

In March 1983, 9.8 million families were principally supported by women who were divorced, separated, widowed, or never married. This is sixteen percent of all families in the United States.[13]

A 1983 Bureau of the Census report projected that jobs for women would accelerate, then experience a continued but slower rise.[14]

RECONCILING ATTITUDES

In the professions persons not considered appropriate have been kept out, and this definitely applied to women in security management. This has begun to change. It is not a new phenomenon to have women in security line management positions, but there are relatively few women who have been managers for more than ten years.

Many men still feel uncomfortable with women in traditional male jobs, but a new set of values is slowly emerging. Many of us still have not adjusted well to women in higher levels of management unless the woman is older. Interactions with men improve as the woman manager ages. Most men in male-intensive professions still do not want to report to a woman, especially if she is younger than he is.[15]

We still spend much of our time seeking ways to simply be ourselves in pursuing the limits of our potential as human beings. By biological design, we are different from one another. Even if we could be the same, I doubt that we would choose to do so. With the wide range of differences between men and women in attitudes based on gender, heredity and envi-

172

ronment, our similarities nevertheless far outweigh our differences.

As more women become clearer about the direction of their career lives, men will be better able to respond. Today we are going through a tremendous transition because of the feminist movement. Some women resent traditional courtesies such as men opening doors, yet other women expect these courtesies. Men are often unsure how to react when they can be criticized for being either chauvinistic or ill-mannered.

Women who can work effectively and harmoniously in spite of being in the minority, and who do not push too hard for acceptance will fare far better. Women in security have greater visibility simply because they are still in the minority. If qualified, they get greater notice than men of similar capability. Likewise, if they do not do a good job, they get higher visibility than men who do not do a good job.[16]

Many of us still regard certain jobs as being either women's or men's work, but we are getting less concerned about the acceptability of what we really want to do. In November 1983 women were on the payroll of every type of employment including heavy construction, lumber and wood products, metal industries, machinery, electronic, and transportation, including guided missiles and space vehicles.[17] They are gaining employment in almost every area of security, and are capable of working with technical electronic security systems, computers, construction, architecture, and any other field that they decide is worthy of the time and energy to learn. A willingness to learn is the key to success in any field.

In the past, few women have been involved in professional associations and were not appointed to important committees or placed at high levels of decision-making. This is changing, and will continue to change as qualified women join the security field.

Many women have difficulty dealing with the camaraderie of predominantly male associations, and exclude themselves from participation. The reality of a male-intensive profession is that men are not accustomed to sharing ideas with women, but many men are willing to exchange information and solutions when given the opportunity.[18] There is strength in the combined efforts of men and women working toward the betterment of the profession through leadership in their professional society.

GOALS FOR 1990

In 1995, 95.3 percent of men age 25-54 will be participating in the work force and 78.7 percent of the women.[19]

The successful woman executive of the future must be flexible enough in her thinking to be receptive to the rapidly changing business environment. She must be able to learn quickly and have the ability to delegate and set up necessary controls.

Women managers and executives of tomorrow will require continuing education and retraining for changing employment needs. Women in security should strive to become Certified Protection Professionals. Current information will be obtained through various professional society education programs such as offered by the American Society for Industrial Security, information retrieval systems, college courses, publications on security subjects, and through information stored in the minds of colleagues. The demand for security books and information will accelerate dramatically as the security field continues to grow.

Businesses as well as persons with home computers will want to access current statistics and research on security. In the future, more courses and information will be provided through the television set: purchases, crime reports, books, legal advice, and security industry news. Booz Allen & Hamilton predict that services through television will be a $30 billion business by the mid-1990s.[20]

To be successful in the future, women leaders must be capable of launching new programs and changing the way the organization operates. Timing those changes is critical to success. Women must have the vision and ability to build a set of shared values, behavior, and common goals within the organization.[21]

As leaders they need charisma and the ability to understand

human behavior, and many women possess these qualities. They must know organizational structure and behaviors within an organization, and learn how to deal with different people and the talents that they bring to the organization. If women can make decisions, they can manage. If they can motivate others into action, they can lead.

According to a *Fortune Magazine* article, good leaders handle people well. Good leaders are not hypercritical of themselves, and they do not let the aggressiveness of others occupy their time and energy or keep score of other's transgressions. They find constructive ways to resolve their anger and guilt, and do not wait to retaliate. The best leaders have confidence in their own competence, and have confidence in others. Getting the job done is more important to a good leader than how he/she appears to others.[22]

BY THE YEAR 2000

The security field will change as a result of women in management positions in much the same way as politics will change as more women become senators and governors, and eventually Vice President and President of the United States. The security profession of the future will develop a greater awareness of behavioral science because women will place more emphasis on concern for individuals within the organization. The public image of security will gradually change from one of policing to one of protection and assistance.

One of women's biggest challenges will be to try to rise above the resistance encountered in working in a traditional male profession. This requires flexibility and confidence in the evolution of our changing social structure. There are risks involved in undergoing change, but the risks of criticism and failure are inherent in leadership roles. The greatest enemy of leadership is fear, and fear of failure will be one of the greatest challenges for women to overcome. After some women are hired into top security management positions, the comfort zone will be established and others will follow.

By the turn of the century, women will be managing areas

of security for which no job descriptions exist today. The demand for services and information will provide a large portion of the new jobs. Information security in a computerized society will require controls not yet developed, and top management will give more attention to the protection of technical data and proprietary information.

Companies need more ongoing security training now, so teaching and staff development will increase. Women will also have greater opportunities to teach college-level security courses.

The engineering field is a male-intensive profession, and the need for engineers will continue into the year 2000 and beyond. Engineers as security professionals will be in demand, and is a good field for women who possess a scientific, mathematical, and mechanical aptitude. The greatest demand will be for electrical and mechanical engineers.[23]

Only a small proportion of jobs created between now and 1995 will be in high technology industries.[24] Service-producing industries such as transportation, communications, public utilities, real estate, and others are projected to account for 75 percent of all new jobs between 1982 and 1995.[25]

Jobs will open up as small businesses, and state and local governments make progress in solving their own problems because they are too diverse for the federal government. States are taking it upon themselves to handle organized crime and regulating hazardous waste, and states with common interests will join together to accomplish their objectives.[26]

There will be advances in the treatment of diseases and illnesses. Health care security will expand to serve a longer-living population, and a society more conscious of well-being.

For at least the next decade the desired behavior traits will be based largely on the male personality, but changes in management style will come about slowly as the role model undergoes transition. However, the successful woman in security will not have to relinquish her femininity in order to an effective leader. As more women are employed in positions as directors or vice presidents of security, there will be greater acceptance of perceived feminine qualities such as understanding, affection, and nuturing. We are dealing with these qualities already, but we call them feedback, recognition, and assistance.

Understanding the human brain and individual personalities will make the security professional's job more effective and less stressful. Women will bring natural talents of intuitiveness to understanding the security organization.

SOME OBSTACLES FOR WOMEN

Some people view women in the work force as contributing to economic crisis because they drive up the unemployment rate for men. One solution is for married women to return to the traditional role of wife and mother at home. This is not a popular solution for the career-oriented woman. However, our society does experience swings in attitude, and a return to views held during the 30s will appeal to those who view women in the labor force as responsible for many of society's problems.[27]

Concern for latchkey children (school children who let themselves in to an empty house while parents work) will gain more attention, and bring pressure and burdens of guilt to working mothers.

Slow economic growth in the 80s and a reduction in administrative work as a result of computers could return married women to the home voluntarily or involuntarily. However, other opportunities will be available to women with the necessary education and the ability to retrain for new jobs.

There is concern for a declining middle class where there will be fewer management jobs at the top and many low paying jobs at the bottom. If some futurists are correct, this will limit the number of desirable jobs for women in security.

THE FUTURE — A SPIRIT OF FREEDOM

Think about and prepare for the future but live now. We all need to be positive contributors to change and learn to cope with change and the turning points of life. We need to try to be satisfied with today while trying to improve for tomorrow. In *Changepoints,* Joyce Landorf refers to the "When and Then" syndrome forces which can overtake our lives. When I make $85,000 a year, then I will be satisfied with my pay. When I become Vice President of Security, then I will feel that I am treated fairly. If this philosophy is used throughout our lives, we never quite find happiness because our aspirations change or perhaps are never met.[28] "If you live your life fully in the present, it can be abundantly rich. If you live it in the past or future, it can be torture."[29]

Our country is, and will continue to be, stronger because of the aspirations of career-oriented women. The talents and potential of women are too valuable a resource to waste.

1. Kissel, Theodore S., *Job Power Money Power for Today's Woman,* UIS Publishing, new Jersey, 1976.
2. Statistical Abstract of the United States, 103rd Edition, 1982-83, U. S. Department of Commerce, Bureau of the Census.
3. Naisbett, John, *Megatrends,* Warner Books, Inc., New York, 1984.
4. Kirkpatrick, Jeane J., *Political Woman,* Basic Books, Inc., Publisher, New York, 1974.
5. Loring, Rosalind K. and Herbert A. Otto, *Life Options,* McGraw-Hill, Inc., New York, 1976.
6. Burrow, Martha G., *Developing Women Managers: What Needs to Be Done?* AMA Report, New York, 1978.
7. Business Intelligence Program, SFI International, Datalog File No. 83-813, *Changing Demographic Patterns in the 1980s,* Menlo Park, CA., 1983.
8. Ibid.
9. Burrow, Martha G., *Developing Women Managers: What Needs to Be Done?* AMA Report, New York, 1978.
10. Business Intelligence Program, SFI International, *Two Income Families; A New Portrait,* Research Report 625, Menlo Park, CA. 1979.
11. *Monthly Labor Review,* Bureau of Labor Statistics, "Occupational Employment Projections Through 1995," Nov. 1983.
12. Business Intelligence Program, SRI International, *Two Income Families; A New Portrait,* Research Report 625, Menlo Park, CA, 1979.
13. Bureau of the Census, March, 1983.
14. *Monthly Labor Review,* Bureau of Labor Statistics, "The 1995 Labor Force: A Second Look," November, 1983.
15. Epstein, Cynthia Fuchs, *Woman'e Place,* University of California Press, Berkeley, Los Angeles, and London, 1970.
16. Ibid.
17. Naisbitt, John, *Megatrends,* Warner Books, Inc., New York, 1984.
18. Epstein, Synthia Fuchs, *Woman's Place,* University of California Press, Berkley, Los Angeles, and London, 1970.
19. *Monthly labor Review,* Bureau of Labor Statistics, "The 1995 Labor Force: A Second Look," November, 1983.

20. *Fortune Magazine,* "Coming Fast: Services Through the TV Set," November 14, 1983.
21. Appelbaum, Eileen, *Back to Work,* Auburn House Publishing Co., Boston, 1981.
22. *Fortune Magazine.* "Corporate Leaders," May 30, 1983.
23. *Monthly Labor Review,* Bureau of Labor Statistics, "Occupational Employment Projections Through 1995," November, 1983.
24. *Monthly Labor Review,* Bureau of Labor Statistics, "High Technology Today and Tomorrow: Small Slice of Employment, November, 1983.
25. *Monthly Labor Review,* Bureau of Labor Statistics, "The Job Outlook Through 1995: Industry Output and Employment," November, 1983.
26. Kirkpatrick, Jean J., *Political Woman,* Basic Books, Inc., New York, 1974.
27. *Fortune Magazine,* "Coming Fast: Services Through the TV Set," November 14, 1983.
28. Landorf, Joyce, *Changepoints,* Fleming H. Revell Co., Old Tappan, New Jersey, 1981.
29. Bry, Adelaide, *Learning to Love Forever,* Macmillan Publishing Co., Inc., New York, 1982.

14

Fire Protection
and Environmental Safety

Glenn S. Gately, CPP

Assistant Director

Casualty-Property Claim Department

The Travelers Insurance Companies
"Honest thinkers are always stealing from each other."
O. W. HOLMES

As the quality of environment rises or falls, so will the quality of life for man.

It was during the late 1960's that concern over environment and safety in the working place culminated in the passage of the Occupational Safety and Health Act of 1970. This concern has been accelerated in the late 1970's and early 1980's by the problems created by asbestos, Agent Orange, dioxanes and other chemicals and materials with resultant nationwide publicity focusing the public's close attention upon any project or development that would appear to negatively impact the environment. The National Environmental Policy Act of 1969 generated the organization of the Environmental Protection Agency in 1970.

Surely the injuries, death and diseases that have occurred not only in the workplace but throughout the span of every day living, have become of prime concern to people everywhere. Life, with all of its advancements, is far more complicated today than it was 25 or 50 years ago. The turn of the next century will find life far more complicated than that surrounding us today. Man will continue to develop ways to improve life but, as is the case with most progress, there will be unwanted side effects. Man made materials will continue to substitute for natural products, many of which are becoming depleted quite rapidly. These substitutive products may be as durable (or more so), strong (or stronger) and generally less expensive than the natural products they replace. But they will be produced only through utilization of processes and material that will, themselves, cause a depletion of natural resources - clean air, pure water and safe ground. Unless brought under control, manufacturing plants will belch forth noxious gases and smoke to foul the air, workers and others will become exposed to chemical components which may bring about respiratory illnesses, debilitating skin rashes and other medical problems. Waste disposal has become a serious environmental headache leading, in some cases, to the abandonment of entire neighborhoods that have become uninhabitable because of the improper disposal of dangerous chemicals.

Fire has been a vital part of man's environment since its discovery. Used to cook food, provide warmth, temper and form metals and for a myriad of other uses, it has also been employed to destroy lives and property. Accidental and intentional fires have increased to dangerous proportions. No planning for improvement in environmental safety in the years to come can overlook the element of fire which will be with us in the next century in the same form as it has for centuries past. Though fire itself will remain the same, the methods of prevention and suppression will change - and improve. We have witnessed the development of advanced sophistication in alarm and suppression systems during the past ten years as well as the progress in producing fire retardant materials to contain the fire. It should be noted in passing, that some of the materials, though fire resistant, have created their own set of problems because of the smoke and noxious fumes that they generate during a fire.

The coming years to the turn of the millenium, will witness advances in the area of environmental protection that will completely overshadow anything that we've witnessed in the past. These advancements will be born of pure necessity because it has become patently evident that we can no longer afford the luxury of dismissing the environmental impact in our constant search for improvements in our daily lives. Thus, the best scientific minds and facilities will be supplemented by sufficient manpower and money to insure that all future advancements, whether in material goods or processes, do not adversely affect man's most precious resources - air, water and land.

Environmental safety will not fall into place by itself nor does each technological advancement carry its own built-in safeguards. Engineers John Heer and Joseph Hagerty, in their book "Environmental Assessments and Statements"[1] offer the case of the Aswan High Dam in Egypt, as an example. Built in the 1960's to produce power and aid agriculture, it stabilized water which gave rise to a small worm that causes serious disease and even death, destroyed sardine fishing and nearly wiped out the rich silt that farmers used as fertilizer. Recognizing the probability of adverse environmental impact from such public projects, government agencies in the United States employ the Environmental Impact Statement which mandates full consideration of forseeable consequences to the environment.

The closing years of the Twentieth Century will see a greater employment of this type of future planning with increased public participation in the planning process. A groundswell of public concern and, in some cases, indignation, will bring about emphasis, by other public agencies and private industry, on environmental safety. This emphasis, and the ensuing effort, will be highly publicized which, in turn, will create a still greater demand for participation by the public during the years to come.

Fire, of both accidental and intentional origin, will continue to be a problem of great concern. The years leading to the turn of the century will witness improvements in alarm and suppression systems. One of the best systems to fight and contain fire is already in place, and has been for a number of years. The past few years have witnessed an expansion of sprinkler systems in buildings open to the public but the coming years will witness a surge in the implementation of sprinkler systems in private homes of all sizes. The sprinkler outlets will be designed to fit unobtrusively into private homes in a decorative manner that will make them readily acceptable to the public. Since water is not an effective element against all fires (e.g. electrical, grease, gasoline) there will be a continuous need for research and development in the area of cost effective systems in all structures that are all encompassing with respect to types of fires. Research and development will continue in the area of fire resistant materials with emphasis being placed upon the materials' ability to retard smoke and noxious fumes as well as flame. Although we are far from the point where firefighters can be eliminated, alarm and suppression systems will be computer directed in structures open to the public and others, to the point where the safety of the public will be immeasurably improved during evacuation, and automated suppression devices will contain the fire to the general area of origin. This will limit the amount of destruction and provide safe and ready access to firefighters for final suppression. The coming fifteen year period and beyond will witness an improvement in materials, alarm and suppression systems that may well make the wholesale destruction of property and lives by fire, a thing of the past.

Although a totally favorable approach to environmental safety would appear to be a certain bet for the future, two major questions come to mind in this regard:

- How much environmental safety can we afford - and when does it become "overkill"?
- What role will law enforcement and the private security sector play in the environmental arena in the years to come?

The average person breathes approximately 16,000 quarts of air each day. At this rate, continuous exposure to air polluted by stack gas, motor vehicle exhausts, petroleum fumes, etc. is bound to impact a person's health to a greater or lesser degree depending upon exposure. People everywhere are suffering from respiratory ailments today to an extent never before realized. A large percentage of these illnesses can be directly attributed to air pollution. The Clean Air Act was enacted by Congress in 1971 and empowered the Environmental Protection Agency to set standards for any facility that released hazardous substances into the atmosphere. At first blush, this would appear to be highly beneficial but consider the questions raised by U.S. Representative Elwood H. Hillis of Indiana during his appearance before the Subcommittee on Health and Environment on September 22, 1981, when he said, in part:

> In my view, there is one very important concept missing from the Clean Air Act. That concept is the recognition of a point of diminishing returns. . . . In the case of the Clean Air Act, the point of diminishing returns is reached when the cost to society in the loss of industrial capability, jobs, capital and international economic competitiveness is greater than the benefit society gains from improved air.

Representative Hillis suggested that standards be set as to what constitutes safe air, add a margin of safety, and consider anything else as excessive. This premise may be equally true in the case of water pollution.

Here then is the arena for environmental progress in the years to come. Since it has become obvious that the public will not abide a diminution if effort to attain a livable atmosphere nor will unusually high costs in connection with pollution control be acceptable, a great deal of effort will be expended to develop and implement systems designed to strike the best balance between the two. Research and development will produce manufacturing processes, materials, air and water "scrubbers" that are far more efficient and cost much less to operate. It is a goal which must and will be attained. Mankind really has no option!

The future of environmental safety will witness a greater degree of advance planning involving the public, governmental agencies and private industry. Since all sectors have a vital stake in the maintenance of a safe environment, this alone will provide a strong inducement toward self regulation. Nonetheless there will continue to be regulations - and more of them. Many of these regulations will have criminal sanctions. Both public law enforcement and private security sectors will have vital roles to play in creating and maintaining the safe environment of the future. In describing criminalists as scientists specializing in the physical examination aspects of criminal investigation, Dr. G.E. Gantner predicts a very important future for those skilled in this profession:

> I believe that criminalists in the future will have special import in areas affecting the environment of man by means of their special skills in microscopy and evaluation of trace physical evidence; for example. filters routinely collect samples from the work environment and therefore fiber identification in the work space may also properly be the work of the criminalist.[2]

Dr. Gantner goes on to note:

> It is my firm belief that a person trained and skilled in criminalistics will have a very special advantage in the future evaluation of the safety of the work place and the living environment and will assist in preventive measures.[3]

Today, many states and the Federal Goverment have promulgated laws with heavy penalties for the illegal use and disposal of hazardous materials. A number of states have implemented an enforcement branch as an adjunct to their state law enforcement agencies or other appropriate branches of state government. The year 2000 and beyond will witness a proliferation of such specialized units, and specialized they will be because the investigation and prosecution of this type of crime is, and will continue to be very complex. William M. Murphy of the Law Enforcement Division of the Michigan Department of Natural Resources recently observed:

> In an effort to stop the spread and, in turn, hold down the very real dangers involved with violations of the laws regulating toxic materials, some law enforcement and environmental protection agencies are forming special units to investigate and prosecute these violators. Because of the huge scope of the activities, the tremendous complexity of the laws, and the various social, economic, and political forces involved, this task is anything but easy.[4]

The addition of specialists involved in the enforcement area of the public sector will undoubtedly result in the implementation and expansion of this type of specialized discipline in private industry. There is a direct casual relationship. The future years offer a remarkable and exciting future to those security practitioners, both investigative and scientific, who prepare for an environmental specialization by training and experience.

As it has in other areas of security today, private industry will aggressively pursue all avenues leading to a safe and secure environment for its employees, its customers and the public. This will necessitate the creation of staff functions in the environmental specialty on their side of the house.

Progress in the area of environmental and fire safety will not come easily or swiftly - but come it will! Because of the cost in manpower and money, it may well take until the end of this century for a workable, cost-effective and enforceable system to be in place, but a safe and healthy environment in which to live is far too important to disregard. In the final analysis - everyone's life depends upon it!

Ms. Mary Ann Snyder, Environmental Claim Unit, Casualty-Property Claim Department, The Travelers Insurance Companies has reviewed the complete article and approves its accuracy and interest.

Glenn S. Gately, CPP is Past Chairman of the Fire Prevention & Safety Committee of the American Society for Industrial Security.

1. John F. Heer,Jr. and D. Joseph Hagerty, "Environmental Assessments and Statements"; Van Nostrand Reinhold Co., New York (1977)
2. G.E.Gantner, MD, "Concern for the Quality of Life and Future Importance of the Forensic Sciences (The Living and Working Environment)"; *Journal of Forensic Sciences,* Vol. 25, No. 4, October 1980.
3. Ibid.
4. William M. Murphy, "Enforcing Environmental Laws - A Modern Day Challenge" *F.B.I. Law Enforcement Bulletin,* November 1983.

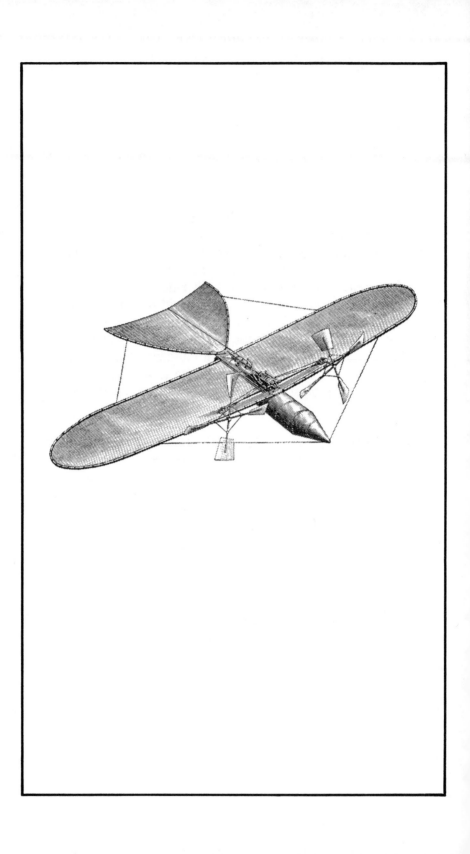

15

Airline Security in the Year 2000

Kenneth C. Moore, CPP

Corporate Security Representative

United Airlines

"Misappropriation of goods or services of any magnitude will necessitate defeating one or more computers."
DR. JOHN M. CARROLL

I am continually impressed by both the differences among the various fields of security and loss prevention and their similarities. The security problems inherent in the airline industry are different than those that one involved in hospital security might encounter, for example. Yet anywhere cash is handled, there will be those who try to steal it. Where there is an opportunity for fraud, there will be those who attempt to take advantage of it. This chapter deals with some of the security problems in the airline industry and ways of overcoming those problems or reducing their impact by the year 2000.

The product we sell in the airline industry is transportation from point A to point B; a seat on an airplane, if you will. In the course of the travel, we may rent you a headset to listen to the movie, sell you a drink and provide a meal. We'll also check your bags for you and deliver them to you at your destination. It seems like a simple enough procedure, yet the security implications are mind boggling.

The airline security investigator on that same flight is wondering if the money collected by the flight attendant for the liquor sales and headset rentals is going to end up in the company coffers or in the flight attendant's pocket or purse. Will the bag a passenger checked in be pilfered or stolen? Is the man across the aisle traveling on a legitimate ticket for which the airline has received revenue? Some passengers may be traveling on counterfeit tickets, altered tickets, stolen tickets, tickets fraudulently ordered by mail and never paid for or tickets ordered over the phone using a legitimate credit card number fraudulently obtained without the owner's knowledge. Will the video cassette for the movie being shown on the flight be stolen by a passenger or crew member before landing? How many pillows, blankets, life vests and silverware will be lost on this flight? Did any of the passengers bring on board their own headsets to avoid the rental fee? Will any of these passengers file a fraudulent baggage claim when they arrive, stating they lost a bag when in fact they did not? Will the air freight shipment of theft prone personal computers a crew member saw being loaded get to the consignee as a complete shipment?

And back on the ground, is anyone stealing cartons of steaks from the flight kitchen? Is there a drug problem among the mechanics who overhaul and repair the aircraft? Are critical, expensive aircraft parts and avionics equipment being stolen and fenced on the used aircraft parts market?

Will we have all these problems solved by the year 2000? Not unless mankind decides to follow the Golden Rule and live their lives with honor and integrity. Failing that, there will always be job security for the security professional. There are, however, some things that can be done which could make a significant impact on losses.

Much of our activity is directed toward various crimes and fraud related to airline tickets. If airline tickets, per se, were totally eliminated, much of the opportunity for this criminal activity would disappear with it. The approach is unique. Instead of protecting the target, you eliminate it. Thus, I would first and foremost, hope for the elimination of the airline ticket by the year 2000. We are already at a point in business transactions where computer entries have replaced much paper documentation. There is really no reason that the airline ticket as a document could not be eliminated.

Look for a moment at the effect on the industry. An altered

ticket usually is accomplished by purchasing a short haul ticket, such as from Los Angeles to San Diego and changing the routing to Los Angeles to New York or London. The real thieves buy children's tickets and are out even less cash. Counterfeit tickets are printed and used or sold. If there were no tickets, but perhaps only an indication on a computer's records that passage had been paid for, this type of crime could be eliminated.

Then there are tickets by mail, where the airline accepts your reservation over the phone, mails you a ticket and asks that you mail them a check. Individuals who work this fraud often order numerous tickets from several airlines in a short period of time, usually under different names but generally to be mailed to the same address. They stay in one location only long enough to get the tickets and then hit the street selling them in bars, barbershops, and service stations. Eliminate the ticket and you eliminate this type of theft.

A related fraud gaining in popularity is the prepaid ticket authorization, where an individual obtains a legitimate name and credit card number from a discarded tissue on a prior transaction and then calls the airline, ordering the ticket charged to that credit card. Depending on the system devised to replace the airline ticket, some or all of this type of fraud could be stopped.

Travel agencies are victims of burglaries and armed robberies in order to obtain tickets and validations plates. Eliminating the ticket would eliminate this type of crime and many other travel agency fraud and defalcation schemes.

An interim step in the elimination of the ticket may be the Automated Ticket and Boarding Pass (ATB), which is a ticket with encoded information on a magnetic strip. Other cards or tickets store data by means of laser readable bar stripe codes, magnetic codes and even the "smart card" which contains its own computer chip and carries a running debit balance in the card. One new laser card reportedly carries 12 million characters; the equivalent of 15,000 pages of information, on the stripe on the card.

The various videotex services are now in their infancy. These are the Value Added Networks or VANS, which is an industry forecasted to reach 30 million homes by 1995 and to be a $35 billion business. Videotex systems such as The Source, owned by Reader's Digest and CompuServe, open up new worlds of access to subscribers who have personal computers in their home.

As it relates to the travel industry, however, subscribers can now check flight schedules and do trip planning on their home computers. Some air carriers are already well into plans which will allow subscribers to make their own airline reservations. Other carriers are taking a more studied view; their particular concern being the potential abuse and damage that could be done by a "hacker," booking phantom reservations, or perhaps ordering tickets to be mailed to them. A great deal of security planning will be necessary to prevent these abuses, but if this method of arranging travel proves to be attractive to the consumer, then that planning will have to be accomplished.

We see then, a new "law" of security and loss prevention: As new marketing and production methods are developed through new technology, commensurate new opportunities for fraud occur. It is a constant challenge of the security industry to not only keep abreast of these changes, but to stay ahead of them. What is frightening is that the potential for fraud appears to be greater through the use of computers, particulary with the drive to make software more "user friendly."

The videotex evolution or revolution will also present problems in protection of proprietary data. Some companies already have replaced numerous manuals and publications with computer stored data which can be retrieved and read by anyone with a terminal. This reduces costs for printing and distribution of manuals and makes it less costly to update policies and changes, since these changes can be made in the computer text rather than printing and distributing new pages. Such items as personnel policies and procedures, price lists, catalogs, emergency prodecures, engineering specifications, travel schedules and computer aided instruction are already transmitted to employees of some firms by videotex rather than the printed page. The airlines have been using similar systems for some time, but its use has largely been restricted to reservations centers where the agent can pull up the daily briefing, find out the ferry schedule in Hong Kong, what shows are playing in Las Vegas or New York, or ski conditions on the slopes. Then when videotex is finally capable of displaying voice and full motion video, its capabilities for training and teaching increase dramatically.

With employees and perhaps other individuals able to obtain access to a wealth of information, extensive security plans will be required to restrict or compartmentalize the information so that only those with a need to know will have access to it.

Videotexing also allows for telecommuting, a new word which describes a worker who stays at home instead of going to the office and works out of his or her home by means of a computer hooked up to the office. It has been estimated that as many as 20 million Americans won't have to go to the office on a regular basis by the year 2000 because of telecommuting. Security problems? You bet!

Baggage theft and pilferage is another serious problem within the airline industry. Much of the pilferage activity occurs within the belly pits of narrow body aircraft. An employee working in the belly pit of an aircraft is there alone and has ample opportunity to open and steal from many bags. Often his helper outside at the belt loader will be serving as a lookout. Containerization of baggage on wide body aircraft has helped to reduce but not eliminate pilferage. It has little effect on baggage theft. Theft and pilferage also occur in other areas such as bag make up areas and containerization will not totally solve the problem.

Innovative approaches will be needed, such as concealed CCTV in the belly pit or the banding of bags at check-in. The CCTV has not yet been tried and the banding only on a limited scale. A device capable of banding bags at the check-in counter so the bag cannot be opened without breaking the seal would be necessary. The banding would have to stay intact through rough handling, but yet be easily removeable by the passenger at destination.

Part of the solution may also relate to the redesign of luggage. Airline baggage experts working with luggage manufacturers should develop new types of locks less susceptible to tampering and openable only by the owners, perhaps by means of electronic codes. The combination lock on luggage has been an advantage to the passenger over the key lock, since keys to most luggage are in the possession of many baggage handlers.

Mandatory 100% screening has been in effect since 1973 and has been successful in reducing the incidence of hijackings. They do continue, however, and now that the seed has been planted in the minds of those who want to gain media attention, who are mentally deranged, or who want to escape from oppression or return to it, as in the case of the "homesick" Cubans, we will continue to have hijackings. Even as improvements in the state of the art allow a smoother, less obtrusive screening and yet a more thorough one, refinements in manpower and human factors will continue to improve the system. I would anticipate that one of these changes will be less need for law enforcement presence at the airport as long as a reasonable response capability exists.

Improvements to the x-ray screening of carry-on luggage will occur through x-ray absorption techniques, which is an automatic computer bases analysis of the size, shape and x-ray density of luggage contents.

By the year 2000, the screening procedure will most probably encompass unobtrusive explosives detection apparatus for both passengers and checked luggage. Considerable research has already been accomplished, primarily as a result of research and development grants from FAA. Several approaches have been explored including vapor detection, decompression sampling, nuclear magnetic resonance (NMR), thermal neutrons and x-ray flourescence. Explosives in luggage are not easily detectable by x-ray and checked luggage is screened only by a fairly reliable profile.

As has always been the case, innovation in approach to difficult problems is essential to their solution. One air carrier, plagued by the loss of over $100,000 worth of life vests, blankets and other property in one year, installed an electronic article surveillance system, identical to that used in stores to detect shoplifters. Sensitized strips fastened to the life vests alarmed the device as passengers exited the jetway, allowing the company to recover 200 of their life vests, worth $6,000 in a six month period. Innovation is both the challenge and the source of satisfaction for the security professional.

There will be an increasing need for security professionals to be of assistance to each other as we attack problems. As an example, if the air carriers are encountering security problems relating to various marketing incentive programs featuring coupons, certificates and passes, we should not feel hesitant to call upon a colleague who specializes in a related field, such as coupon security, for advice. Similarly, we need to turn to specialists in CCTV, alarm systems and access control as well as other fields. The state of the art is changing too rapidly for the "general practitioner" to keep abreast. To be a jack-of-all-trades and master of none in the security field is no longer adequate. corporate management is entitled to expect more from us.

Kenneth C. Moore is the author of *Airport, Aircraft and Airline Security* , published by Butterworth Publishers.

16

College Security: A Look At the Past, the Present and the Future

Lawrence J. Fennelly

Harvard University Police

"Certain Crimes Will Always Prevail
WILLIAM F. FORD

Introduction

This chapter on "College Security: A Look at the Past, the Present, and the Future" is based on actual fact. A survey on crime on the college campus was conducted in 1985. In doing a survey on crime on the college campus, I should explain that this information is based on a rather simple form that was filled out by participants who attended security seminars on "Crime Prevention Strategies on the College Campus." Sixty-five percent of the participants were directors of security departments at colleges and universities, and the remainder were assistant directors, administrative personnel and law enforcement personnel. Those who filled out the questionaire were from both large and small colleges. The single factor that emerged from the survey is that all participants have the same problems and concerns, whether they come from a large college with a staff of 35 or over or from a small community college with a staff of six.

These crime problems will still be with us in the year 2000. In looking into the future some strategies are layed out that will set directions for the management of college campuses.

How Campus Law Enforcement Started - The Past

It was not our intent to do any kind of in-depth study of offenses versus population, but rather to identify specific problems. Many agreed that crime has increased, as has the reporting of crime increased.

Campus law enforcement goes back to the seventeenth century at Harvard University when a Cambridge constable and six guards protected the Harvard Yard, and at Yale back to 1894 when two New Haven police officers volunteered to patrol the Yale campus and were later hired by Yale University. In 1914, William Weiser, Chief of Police at Yale, wrote in his book *Yale Memories,* "The most important function was to protect the students, their property and the University property." If he were alive today, I am sure he would include "employees and their property." In six years, campus policing will be 100 years old. Many colleges have grown over the years in improving their method of operation. Some have full police authority and some will never have it. Some give new employees 14 to 21 weeks training in a municipal police academy . . . and some give two days training, a flashlight and the keys.

Campus law enforcement has come a long way in the past 25 years. This is due primarily to a new breed of professional thinkers and achievers working in this field.

Identifying Crime Problems on the College Campus 1985 - The Present

The survey results have also been broken down into the three categories, which are the students', the colleges', and the security directors' concerns. In addition, a partial comparison of problems and concerns were made with the private corporate sector.

Section A: Student Category

In doing the Survey of Crime Problems on the College Campus, 1985, I found that the #1 crime problem is the theft of students' property such as purses, wallets, knapsacks (Containing credit cards and identification cards), from dining halls, libraries, dormitories and athletic facilities. This property generally is left unattended and unsecured. The next four items could possibly be labeled item #2 depending on what part of the country is involved.

1. Theft of jewelry and cameras from the students' residence or dormitory. These thefts generally occur because the room is unlocked and unoccupied.
2. Breaking and Entry into a motor vehicle, and larceny of such items as:
   - hub caps
   - radios
   - tape decks
   - batteries
   - general vandalism
   - the actual theft of the vehicle.
3. Bicycle thefts, specifically ten speed bikes which are secured with poor quality locks or chains.
4. Students stealing from students:
   - in the dormitory
   - problems with out-of-state athletes who come on campus for various sport events.
5. Theft of coats and books.

Section B

1. Alcohol and drug abuse, two items which are of major concern to the college administration. Many in the survey agreed that after heavy drinking on the campus came vandalism to college property.
2. Violent crime, sexual assault, acquaintance rape, unreported rapes, assaults, harassment and obscene phone calls was the next ranking group of concerns. One college reported prostitution as their #1 problem and another reported "peeping Toms" at their women's college.
3. Vandalism of such areas as:
   - in the dormitory/residence halls, and to the grounds
   - laundry machines
   - in the classroom
   - damage to smoke detectors

- graffitti, both interior and exterior, in the bathrooms (and homosexual-related)
- to vending machines
- to windows; breaking
- destruction of signs, in one case caused by junior high students going through the campus.

4. The pulling of fire alarms within dormitories, and false alarms throughout the campus. In addition, fires set in trash chutes and in bathrooms in the dormitories.

Section A: University or College Category

Under this category we are referring to the types of incidences in which the College or University becomes the victim.

1. The #1 item recognized as a crime of the present and the future is theft of the COMPUTER and its components, software and user time.
2. Laboratory equipment, i.e. balance scales and microscopes.
3. Theft of small office equipment not bolted down.
4. Video equipment and visual aids stolen due to lack of key control.
5. Improper handling of large sums of money, either in the bookstore or cafeteria, with no checks and balances of cash flow and inventory.
6. Petty cash thefts.
7. Trespassing.
8. Shoplifting in the bookstore.
9. Forgery of college documents.
10. Theft of college furniture.
11. Slugs used in vending machines.
12. Xeroxed dollar bills in coin changers.
13. Internal theft by current or former employees.
14. Internal theft after 5:00 PM and before 9:00 AM the next day, with no signs of forced entry.
15. The theft of livestock was mentioned in only one case.

Section B - Physical Hardware

Although the four items below are not directly crime-related,

they are of major concern to those in educational institutions.
1. Card access control was a question raised at every seminar. Also, locking devices available to secure computers.
2. Reducing both fire and intrusion false alarms.
3. Key control; 99% of the over 300 colleges agreed they did not have complete key control on their campus. There was a strong interest and concern for keys that could not be duplicated and for removable core cylinders. Theft of keys to buildings is also a problem in a minimum number of areas.
4. Inadequate lighting and how to improve it either for safety and security or for energy management reasons.

Security Directors Category

This is the final category; it is basically a listing of brief concerns.
- Liability factors and lawsuits.
- Lack of policy and procedures manual for the department, and;
   a. no policy on the use of deadly force
   b. policy and procedures for the use of firearms
   c. bomb threats and bomb threat procedures.
- Ratio of law enforcement personnel versus overall college population.
- Thefts and crimes that go unreported.
- Traffic control, parking and traffic violations.
- Getting the administration and faculty to cooperate with the security department.
- Lack of motivation by university personnel (students and faculty) in regard to the protection of their personal property.
- Missing property as a result of inventory which is either lost, misplaced or stolen. However, departments are seeking release of accountability as a result of this inventory.
- Dormitory security, trespassers in dorms, students leaving their rooms unlocked.
- Arresting an employee for stealing VERSUS no arrest and giving the individual a temporary suspension and allowing that person to return to work.

- Many agreed that students who are dealing in drugs should be arrested and prosecuted.
- Campus police don't have proper training and lack proper law enforcement authority to make an arrest.
- One person stated he had no comprehensive master plan concerning security.
- Theft of property by custodial contractors.
- Responding to crisis management problems rather than taking action before the fact.

The same comment was made by many, that their administration wanted a free and open campus. They didn't want crime on the campus, yet would not properly train or equip the security personnel. As an example, one college currently trains *all* their new recruits at a local municipal police academy which they attend for 21 weeks, while in some colleges new recruits receive less that four weeks of training before going out on the street, and in small colleges there is no training.

THE FUTURE

In order for campus security to succeed in the year 2000 the role of the campus police department or protection body will have to be clearly defined. Its reporting structure should come under the direction of the institution's Vice President or the University Corporate Counsel at the very least. Non-police duties will have to be eliminated. The principal question to be addressed will be are such staff members the protective body of police officers or are they security guards? The above sentences no doubt will perplex a great number of college administrators. For far too long campus policing has come under non-legal administrative personnel and in many instances beneath the proper level of reporting structure. Frequently the budget for protective services will become part of the total facilities package which includes the full line of maintenance and support functions.

Stage one - Growth

The direction in which campus security should be heading is to position itself ten steps higher than comparable municipal or city police. This should be the first objective or analysis stage in seeking improvement and can be accomplished by a fair assessment of local representative departments. Police authority will have to be equal to, or better than, the particular city or town in which the campus is located. To achieve this goal, we in campus security will have to be trained equally, if not better than the local police constabulary. At present, municipal law enforcement training is approximately 12 to 16 weeks in length, the year 2000 it will expand such training to 20 to 24 weeks. This shall be supported by a three years probationery period as an average. Eighty percent of campus security training will be performed by in-house security personnel and support staff. To attain this level of professionalism necessary to reach parity or better with local municipalities, all of these items must be addressed or accomplished.

Stage two - Increase and Changing Demands

In court room actions, arraignment officers will be prosecuting their own cases as well as acting independently in the arrest and booking of prisoners. Prisoners will be processed by Campus Security Departments initially before city or county jail processing. Arrests will be professionally conducted. Keep in mind hat the trends of municipal departments will effect overall operations.

If cutbacks in funding and manpower are experienced, services will be the first category cut. Campus management at this point will be looking at the overall needs and prioritize all services. How to obtain a safe environment within a campus community at the least cost will be an obvious factor. Stage two will emphasize developing professionalism and achievements based upon performance as an independent service will have been attained.

Stage three

In every campus department, direct patrol as well as others will be utilized as contributing to the overall loss prevention program. Each department will have a fully trained crime prevention specialist who will integrate his program jointly with the campus community and appropriate protection services. Each of these will have a part to play in the overall success of an effective prevention program. Crime Prevention Specialists or technicians will deal with analyzing how it happened and how it could have been prevented? Detectives will traditionally be concerned with identifying who committed the crime and what the motivation was. Patrol officers will be more effectively deployed in areas where specific crimes have occurred or where it is determined they likely occur. And finally, the campus community must be educated by being made aware of potential problems based upon past events and appropriate analysis. The campus population by being responsive will supplement the resources of crime prevention.

Stage Four - Management

This is the stage where management must take a hard look at what kinds and types of training and development are necessary. First we must determine the number of trainers necessary to attain the level of professionalism we seek. Detectives, for example, should enroll in advance courses in criminal and constitutional law (re-certification requirements given annually). The principal managers in command should be required to attend high level teaching facilities such as the Southern Police Institute and the national Crime Prevention Institute . . . take courses from the University of Louisville. Other excellent training resources are the FBI Academy and the Advanced Security Management Institutes conducted by the American Society for Industrial Security International. Other key members of the department, as appropriate, will also be developed and molded through various seminars, workshops and academies. Management will be faced with increased demands to identify and resolve potential problems in advance. And to deal with these problems the principal campus enforcement manager must be well trained.

Stage Five - Standards

Candidate selection and promotional advancement will be

by examination only. Highest ranking candidates must then meet outstanding standards of physical and mental health. The process should include a diverse selection committee comprised of internal as well as external members.

Supervisory promotions should be dependent upon appropriate training and development which shall provide and qualify the officer for credible acceptance and in performing his/her job requirements. Higher educational accomplishments shall be increasingly necessary as standards increase for promotional consideration.

The ability to work under stress and to communicate effectively with the faculty, students and administration will be a must.

Stage Six - Technology

We are in an era of extreme technological changes and campus enforcement and protection is no exception to this condition. An integral of any campus Law Enforcement Agency of the future will be its computer capabilities. Computer operations within the law enforcement community is in its infancy. With the impact of new technologies by the year 2000, the use of computers will be as much a part of the "tools of the trade" for a police officer as a nightstick or a flashlight. A Police Information Management System will provide data and capabilities that have never been associated with the criminal justice field. Administratively, it provides a clear, precise up-to-the-minute picture of crime conditions on campus as well as setting a course of corrective action to combat crimes. Most comprehensive in-house computer systems will process form reports that can be distributed in a timely manner to line supervisors and personnel so that an immediate understanding of the problems can be shared by the whole department and campus leadership.

The most effective function of a computer within the campus police department is the records retention capability. The needs and demands of the future will be simplified with the anticipated advancement of the overall application of computer technology in police operations.

Operationally, the role of computer systems will be greatly expanded when used as a method to evaluate the effectiveness of line personnel and specific assignments. A formulated blueprint to guide "directed patrols" and to dispense resource allocations as well as various adjustments to operational orders will be handled through computer analysis. A well managed information system will be the basis of all operational success in a progressive campus law enforcement department by the year 2000.

There are additional capabilities that are just being explored on a start up basis such as crime forecasting, telecommunication linking police departments, and related computer user groups.

These six stages need not be achieved in the order stated to achieve the success that will follow if they are collectively adhered to. This is a long-time plan which will take many years to implement. By the year 2000, the days of being a campus watchman will be over, the unprofessional duties and non police work will become a thing of the past.

Specific requirements and changes that the future may hold are as follows:

- Becoming a campus police officer - Bachelor's Degree
- Training - all sworn officers will be EMT's (Emergency Medical Technicians). Firearms qualifications will be on a monthly basis - Stress management and burnout courses will be necessary. In addition, sensitivity training will be a requirement for all when dealing with the community and for supervisors when dealing with staff in particular. Directive patrol will be an active form of operational procedure.
- Lawyers representing colleges will be working directly with the campus police. They will be addressing specific cases as near to the point of arrest as is possible with the potential for civil liability violation cases which may develop against the particular institution given a priority. The lawyer's presence and expertise will support, assist and protect the campus law enforcement officers in the field, particularly where rape and sexual abuse cases are concerned.

- Campus police will become increasingly more involved with executive protection for dignitaries such as presidential candidates and those individuals who are considered risks. In addition, key faculty members' department for monitoring and will also respond to alarms.
- Court decisions rendered against colleges and universities will force the improvement of prevention and security programs on campus.
- In some instances insurance companies will be establishing program standards for police operations as a result of anticipated law suits against the educational community generally. Physical security standards for dormitories and housing can be expected to be a part of the changes.

Conclusion

The colleges and universities by the year 2000 must be ready to meet the challenges of the future. Security Directors should begin to advise their respective administrations of short and long-range plans for police operations and administrative controls necessary to guide and manage their individual protection services.

The image of campus security has improved over the past 30 years and this positive image is being transmitted to the students, faculty and the public. What will that image look like in fifteen years? Will adminstrators be ready for the challenges of the future and the new technologies of the years ahead?

We must plan now to cost effectively implement modernization and develop the managers to effectively and successfully lead campus security forces.

17

Museum Security in the Year 2000

Gerard Shirar, Chief of Security

Museum of Fine Arts

Boston, MA 02115

"We judge ourselves by what we feel capable of doing, others judge us by what we have done."
LONGFELLOW

INTRODUCTION

The Museum

Misconceptions generally held about museums are that they are drab bastions of scholarly effort, immune to the social and economic forces which impact society in general; that museums are well protected, employing highly sophisticated security measures, and that those who work in the museum world are extremely security minded.

In truth the picture is somewhat different, and while there is danger in generalizing, it is important to the understanding of our subject to look at today's museums, and the direction in which they are headed. Since the future is built on the present, the trends we see today will likely be the standards of tomorrow.

Museums come in all sizes, and themes vary. Although the function of a museum is universal, to educate through the objects in the collection and to preserve these objects for the education of future generations, the bulk of museums are small in size, highly specialized institutions which exist outside the mainstream, as it were, and which feel few of the dynamic forces which influence the course of the larger institutions.

For the purpose of our discussion we shall look at museum security in the year 2000 from the perspective of the large art museum which operates in a major urban setting, whose activities are played out in a wide arena encompassing the immediate community, the nation, and the world. Our selection of the art museum as the focal point of our discussion simply stated is because these institutions have been the trend setters and have far and away been the most dynamic.

For many, the words "art museum" conjure up an image of an imposing building nestled in a park setting where one can spend a rainy Sunday afternoon communing with sculpture and paintings which have occupied the same space for twenty or more years, topping off the visit with a cup of tea, sipped while a string quartet plays in the background.

The tea and string quartet can still be found, but the park setting is often alive with placard carrying demonstrators. Parking and traffic in the area are major problems, and the building swarms with crowds of people on their way to a variety of activities such as to a climate controlled, specially designed exhibition hall housing art treasures on loan from an iron curtain country (this in spite of a problemsome diplomatic climate), to a gourmet four-star rated restaurant, or to a world premier of a film shown in a large capacity modern auditorium. Perhaps some are on their way to attend a reception held by their employer, in a modern function room, catered by the museum's food service staff, or to shop in a large, well appointed retail shop, specializing in the sale of merchandise related to the museum's collection.

Many changes have taken place in the major urban art museum in the past decade which will have a profound effect on how museums will operate, and the philosophy which will guide their development in the future. How and why these changes have taken place can best be explained in terms of the changes which have taken place in society in general.

Museums, like other institutions, are slow to evolve and even slower to accept change. Society moves at a greater pace, and the result frequently is an institution out of step with the times. The past and tradition act as a magnet holding change to a slow, gradual pace. When change does take place, there is a "ripple effect" associated with it. For example, a major museum decides to break with tradition and begins to acquire a photographic collection of contemporary art and organizes a curitorial department to care for it. These acts will have been preceeded by considerable discussion and thought over a long period of time, and while the actions themselves appear suddenly, the process leading to the decision has been gradual. One-by-one other institutions follow suit, and soon what was once innovative or pioneering becomes commonplace.

A term frequently used by those in museum work, "museum world," is an apt descriptor since extensive contact and intercourse exists between the great museums of the world in both scholarly and temporal matters. In addition to informal contact among staffs, a number of national and international organizations act as a "forum" for more formal intercourse.

In recent years the most significant innovations have come from the major art museums in the United States, and it is reasonable to expect that these innovations will find broad acceptance throughout the museum world by the year 2000. Why these changes have occurred forms a backdrop to an understanding of the problems the security manager must face as the century draws to a close.

How We Got There

By the seventies, the major art museums of the United States, many of which were founded in the Victorian era, began to question their relevance to the community they served. The seventies, a time of social unrest, brought into question many time honored traditions and attitudes which had guided these institutions in the past. Financial support was becoming a problem. People with large personal fortunes previously relied on to fund major projects and to support the museum's operations and programs were no longer able to do so. The tax laws, inflations, rising operating costs, and museum employee pressures for better wages and benefits taxes heavily the ability of the wealthy to continue to carry the burden of support. Those museums which drew financial support from public funds provided by the communities in which they were located found this source of funding to be unreliable since, as the debt racked older cities began to cut expenses, museums were the first to feel the pinch. Attendance was dropping in almost direct proportion to the rise in operating costs. Support from the community was not forthcoming since the perception widely held was that art museums were elitest.

A few saw the trends early, and the more farsighted among the larger museums began to chart a new direction, one intended to engender broad based financial support and to bring them back into he mainstream of the community. The new course had to consider both maintaining the solvency of the institution as well as developing the capability to implement programs with broad appeal, within the contraints formed by the basic purpose of the institution. At this time museums began to experience a series of dramatic thefts. The normal reaction, based on past practice, was to cover up losses whenever possible to maintain the institution's reputation; the concern being that losses would jeopardize gifts and loans from other instituions or private individuals. In truth, security in most museums was given only lip service, and a security programs as today's security professional understands the term was nonexistent. The main line of defense was represented by an underpayed, ill-used guard force, comprised mainly of men who had retired from a lifetime of unskilled work. Responsibility for the security of the museum was divided, and when a loss occurred, or another security problem developed, responsibility was hard to fix.

The serious security problems which beset the museums in the seventies had a beneficial effect, as it turned out, since the crisis put pressure on those who decided the institution's direction to solve this long standing problem. The solution lay in a better definition of responsibility and the employment of a manager skilled in the principles and techniques of security. The decision to employ such an individual came at an opportune time since as museums began to launch new programs and activities to implement the outward reach philosophy, security became more complex. Under the leadership of the professional security manager, museum security departments began to play a more expanded role in the operation of their institutions.

The seventies saw the so-called blockbuster exhibit, drawn from the collections of the national museums of Italy, as in the case of Pompeii, and Egypt, in the case of King Tut. These exhibits, with their major crowd control problems, were held within facilities not designed for the vast numbers which had to be accommodated. Successfully coping with these problems required a well organized and motivated professional security force. Unlike sporting events which generally involve one day events, a museum exhibition will last three months or more, with crowd control problems coped with day-after-day. The 1970's saw museum security recognized as an important and necessary function, one that ranked in importance with the other major departments of the museum. Whereas the security force previously had been placed under a Building Superintendent, the Security Manager now reported to the Director, or in the case where the museum had an Associate Director, to the Associate Director for Operations

In one short decade, museum security came of age, concurrent with a revitalization of the concept of the art museum.

Security Problems in the Year 2000

What will the future hold for museum security in the year 2000? First, we can expect the security function to evolve as the museum and its programs evolve since security is a service function most effective when fully integrated with the activities it supports.

The museum security manager will have to be in a strict sense a good manager. Million dollar or more security budgets for the major U.S. art museum is now the norm. Security in an art museum is labor intensive, with 70% or more of the budget represented by salaries. The traditional way of protecting art has been the gallery guard. Those who live intimately with the problem recognize that the guard is perhaps the least effective method of protecting works of art, and in the face of increasing attendance the guard's effectiveness decreases markedly. Other more efficient and cost effective alternatives are available, however, adoption of these methods must prevail against long established perceptions about how art and other objects in a museum must be exhibited. Education appears to be the key to creating a climate for trying new techniques and concepts, with innovation offering the means to lower resistance to change.

Habits die hard in museums and, little by little, esthetically acceptable techniques are being developed to better protect exhibits, with the guard shifting to a supporting, reinforcing role, rather than the primary means. By the year 2000, there will be far fewer guards in an art museum, better trained, with greater reliance placed on physical security measures to protect art objects. The resultant savings can then be directed into other programs.

The presence of the professional security manager will result in a full service security program. Part of that program will be security education, training directed at both the support and professional staff of the museum. Security is an environmental factor, and in order for a security program to be most effective, it must blend with the business being conducted. Those who make a museum work must understand the principles of security as they effect the museum's activities in order that sound decisions can be made. A scholar who aspires to a career in museum work will have made a considerable sacrifice to acquire the knowledge necessary to earn and hold a position on a museum staff. However, this inquiring, gifted mind will turn off when the issue of security is raised.

Security in the museum setting cannot be an add on or an isolated function. The public exhibition of art and other valuable objects must not only consider aesthetics and scholarship, but the safety of the objects as well. A realistic understanding of the threat faced by a museum is fundamental to arriving at ways of meeting that threat. A principle function of a museum is to preserve the objects in the collection. A fundamental part of the preservation process is to protect these objects from vandalism and theft, a function of security. Ultimate responsibility for preservation process, i.e. the security manager, the research lab., the engineering staff (responsible for the operation of the climate control system), etc., merely support. It therefore follows that the scholar who aspires to be a museum curator must make an effort to understand the principles governing these supporting disciplines. There seems to be a growing awareness of this truth among younger curatorial staff members and, if the trend continues, by the year 2000 many of the arbitrary obstacles to providing objects on exhibition with adequate security hopefully will have disappeared.

By the year 2000, we can expect to see new dimensions to the security threat facing the world's museums. The search for the exhibition with great popular appeal will in large measure bring this about. The world's great museums are exio diplomatic in the sense that they deal and negotiate in a world arena, maintain contacts with foreign governments, and governmental entities without the encumbrances and formalities which governments must adhere to. Some of the best exhibition potentials lie in countries with hard political realities attached. There is unfortunately little a museum can do to disassociate itself from the focus of those who have suffered at the hands of a government which has a touring exhibition in the museum. Thus, as a museum follows the course set in the seventies, its administration can expect to deal with many of the world's unpleasant realities.

Terrorism, a growing political phenomenon, will represent a serious threat to the world's major museums, particularly those in the developed democratic countries of the world. A terrorist with a bomb or automatic weapon can put his case on the news media's front pages and TV screens of the free world. The more apalling the target, the greater the opportunity for publicity. Can museums expect to be immune?

Spaceage technology, particulary the computer, has already found application in museum security. Computer assisted alarm systems and closed circuit television are in wide use now. The future will see the introduction of robotics into the museum environment. Robots will patrol the building at night, performing functions of the traditional watchman, without the attendant drawbacks of salary, benefits, absences, and the ever present threat of employee dishonesty. To counteract the employee dishonesty problem, new techniques will be employed. Conventional keys will be replaced by access control systems, using the fingerprint to identify authorized individuals. Access to storage areas will be centrally controlled, using remotely controlled locks.

Records pertaining to the collection will be computerized, permitting an effective audit program not now possible for large collections using a manual record system. with some collections numbering in the millions of objects and with only a relatively small percentage of these objects on exhibition or in use at any one time, the threat of surreptitious theft by employees with access to storage is significant. An aggressive audit program, conducted on an unannounced basis, offers an effective tool in deterring internal theft since the chances are high that a theft from storage would be detected sooner. The computer will permit the use of a statistical model, to randomly select objects for inventory with various degrees of coverage, i.e. a 100% inventory without the need to physically inventory every object.

Employee dishonesty now and in the year 2000 will constitute the greatest security threat. Internal security programs assisted by new security technology will be the key to containment.

As museums attract larger crowds, public safety in the vicinity of the museum assumes greater importance. People will not frequent areas of a city they perceive to be unsafe and, as a consequence, we can expect to see greater involvement on the part of museums with the public safety problem in the area immediately surrounding the institution. The trend of citizen involvement in activities to counteract crime and improve personal safety, which began with the great increase in street crime in the seventies, will continue. Organized neighborhood patrols and crime watches have proven to be effective in reducing the incidents of crime. Involvement with neighborhood crime watch groups on the part of businesses, industry, and educational institutions will also grow. The active support of these organizations has had a sustaining effect on the volunteer groups, resulting in better organization, greater citizen participation, and a longer period of effort. As many museums are located in areas of the city which are in transition and street crime tends to be high, it is a matter of self-interest for them to get involved in and support this aspect of the community's affairs.

As museums seek to hold down costs, many of the functions previously performed by people employed directly by the museum will be contracted out. Food service, coat check, parking, and even security services will be provided by firms specializing in these areas. In order for this to take place safely, internal security measures must be adopted to compensate for the increased threat which the introduction of non-museum employees into the environment imposes.

Contracts covering these services must address periods of building access. Work areas must be designated so that people performing the contract service can do so while physically segregated from access to the galleries, except when the galleries are under guard.

The museum security manager must anticipate this trend, and prepare for the day when even his own staff will in part be employees of a contract service.

An active museum means an active program, with long operating hours to accommodate the activity. An increasing trend is to open parts of the museum building, as opposed to the whole building or collection, particularly in the evening. The areas open usually include the museum restaurant, lecture hall, and special exhibition galleries. Extended hours increases exposure, and requires secure methods to segregate the open portions of the building from the closed, and to maintain surveillance over the collection in the closed areas. New construction should consider the trend toward contracting for services, and the practice of opening parts of the museum building.

The art museum in the year 2000 will be a far different place than it is today, and insofar as one can predict the future, a more challenging place for the security manager.

18

Transportation Security Can We Meet the Challenge of the Future?

John J. Strauchs, CCP

Principal & Associates, Inc.

"Conservative estimates predict that by 1990 we will be producing 17,000 robots per year and that the total robot workforce will reach 80,000. Most experts would double those figures."
JOHN NAISBITT

As bleak as the transportation security picture may appear to be today by some accounts, one of the most probable forecasts which can be made is that necessity will gradually bring about improvement. The need for loss prevention programs and new technology will certainly not abate. The following forecasts, therefore, are not the result of crystal ball gazing, but rather are formed on the basis of projections of current needs, as well as where state of the art in security appears to be going.[1]

Technology Explosion — Computer Revolution

Based on what one can see from current computer technology, by the year 2000 it is very likely that most computers will be talking directly to one another from both ends of the transportation chain, and perhaps en route as well. Cargo will be electronically tracked from the warehouse and loading dock to the end user. It is also probable that by the year 2000, most businesses will be managed by computer. computers at either end will be able to electronically compare notes, making cargo documentation significantly more reliable, accurate, and detailed — all in a "real time" context. Public and commercial transportation, especially public mass transit systems and air carriers, will reap the benefits of automation technology, and will control and monitor the movement and safety of vast numbers of people throughout their networks.

As electronic advances seep into every segment of the corporate world, the transportation industry will change, and along with it, the security field, as well. It is likely that some of the major advances which will benefit transportation security the most may include the following: greater use of robotics, increasingly "smarter" sensors and alarm control panels, improved security systems for remote locations with less reliance on telephone lines and alternating current electrical power, less reliance of metallic telephone lines, virtually complete conversion to fiber optics, more "real-time" security system information for the user, greater use of biometric access control and intrusion detection systems, alarm systems with extremely low false and nuisance alarm rates, increasing use of satellite data communications, alarm system zoning on a point-by-point basis, much greater use of speech synthesizers and user prompting CRT programs, and almost continuous computer self-auditing of systems an system events. Having taken this broad sweep, a brief look at more specific technological changes in the transportation security field is presented in the following:

- Individual item identification will be available for all businesses, large and small, and at reasonable costs. Although aspects of this technology are somewhat available now, they are relatively expensive and do not have universal application. The tracking of cargo, shipments, and even baggage will benefit by improved and cheaper technology. Items may be marked by bar codes which are optically scanned, or by article electronic surveillance tags which would be electronically scanned and tracked. The computers managing these shipments will know what and where each individual item is at virtually all times. Inventories will be accurate, totally comprehensive, and instantaneously available. Perpetual inventories will finally live up to their name.
- Technology will come up with electronic or chemical ways

of tracing or marking shipments — if not items — en route, to aid owner identification in the event that they are lost, damaged or stolen. Ion tracing chemicals, personalized microdot implants, diode implants, and yet-to-be-discovered technologies will make all this possible.

- World-wide and intra-nation tracking of large shipments and carriers will be possible, such as by means of satellite or criss-cross radar technology, both of which will be enhanced from present day standards. Costs for such tracking will fall significantly. Point-to-point monitoring of vehicles on the road will be routine.
- National and international central station services will monitor security systems on a regional, if not global, basis. While this capability is currently available, costs will go down and coverage will be extended. Countries with reliable telephone systems may continue to use digital dialers, which will be "smarter" and more reliable and will have more channels. The growth of satellite communications will make nation-wide central station services more efficient and pervasive. Stations will monitor more and more zones per subscriber. Radio frequency-based systems will experience gradual general acceptance, as well as acceptance from fire protection and life-safety code authorities.
- Volumetric intrusion detection systems will see broader use for warehouse and maintenance operations. The shifting of merchandise in a typical warehouse has often made it difficult to use volumetric sensors since the merchandise often blocks viewing zones. Special sensors for warehouse applications will be developed, such as greater use of overhead sensing techniques and "blanketing/flooding" sensing techniques. In the future false and nuisance alarm rates will go down dramatically. There will be greater variety in outdoor sensors. Significant improvements in motion detection on closed-circuit television — including outdoors — will realize significant use in the transportation industry. Other improvements will be far more reliable passive infrared sensors; microwave and ultrasonic sensors will take a back seat.
- There will be an increasing use of radio-signal based

(wireless) systems, especially for remote locations. Many more of these systems will be recognized by approving and testing authorities. Range, numbers of zones, reliability, and immunity to interference will be improved. These systems will be fully supervised. Remote locations will have options for solar energy power sources. Batteries will become more efficient.[2]

• Reliable biometric and "individualized" intrusion detection and access control systems will find significant applications for the transportation industry. These systems rely on either the human attributes of specific persons or utilize devices carried by authorized persons which carry each persons "signature." It will be possible to monitor large numbers of authorized persons over large areas. These systems will work indoors and outdoors. Some will not require doors for access control. Variations of such systems already exist, but they are relatively expensive and canot presently accommodate large numbers of persons or large areas of coverage. "Cycle-through" times for persons for contemporary biometric access control systems are unacceptably long; future systems will cut these times dramatically.

United States Government

The United States Government will re-involve itself in transportation and cargo security. The Federal Government will eventually see that it is not presently fulfilling its role and will re-establish it's involvement, possibly to a greater extent than in the past. Laws will be passed which regulate transportation security to some extent, despite initial objections from the transportation industry and corporate America. Crime incident reporting will become mandatory for selected types of cargo. Federal involvement is likely to expand in all areas, not just with the United States Department of Transportation. The Department of Transportation will, however, continue to be the leader. The United States Justice Department could conceivably establish an office for transportation crimes. The United States Coast Guard, Navy, and other interested agencies will initiate major efforts to stem piracy and smuggling, including on the High Seas. Strict governmental controls for international air carriers suspected of illegally transporting narcotics (especially carriers with routes in South America) will be implemented.

It is likely that there will be greater efforts made at collecting intelligence related to transportation crime, with a commensurate growth in the United States Government's willingness to share this information, both nationally and internationally. On an international basis, there will be greater international cooperation and interdependence in transportation security, especially in maritime cargo and air travel. An international body will be established for international transportation and cargo security.

Western Europe

It would be difficult to point to any dramatic differences in transportation security between the United States and Western Europe. Certainly, the political problems one observes in the European Economic Community are disturbing and it appears to be a safe assumption that inter-nation transportation security will suffer as a result. At one time, one could have also been concerned that Western Europe — in a generalized sense — was lagging far behing in state-of-the-art security technology. Today, this is less certain as England, West Germany, France and Italy are making bold progress in catching up with American security technology, and even equalling or surpassing the United States in certain specialized systems. Whatever gaps may exist will narrow in the coming years.

Crime Patterns

As the result of major breakthroughs in cargo control and accountability at the warehouse resulting in loss reduction, crime statistics are likely to show a shift to the manufacturing site or the retail outlet or end user. It is not so much that crime at these locations will dramatically increase, but rather that more and more previously undetected incidents will be reported. Mandatory reporting and improvements in reporting capabilities will result in more losses being reported. For a while, over all cargo crime statistics may appear to go up despite the growth in security capabilities and effectiveness. In fact, crime may be going down, but the industry's greater abilities to detect criminal incidents will make it seem that crime is increasing. Further, the percent of crime attributable to "insiders" is likely to increase.

Transportation Security Administration and Management

Due to significantly expanded specialization in the security profession (such as the emergence of "security engineering" as a registered service by the year 2000), companies will use many more outside services. It will be unrealistic to expect security directors to know and do everything. It is probable that investigations, security personnel recruitment and screening, security system installation, security engineering, auditing, inventory, guard operations (especially outside posts), computer programming for security departments, and central station monitoring will be increasingly contracted out to service firms. Only the corporate giants will be able to afford to provide these capabilities internally and even they will contract out for more services than they do today. In-house security departments will be given mostly managerial responsibilities. At the same time, these departments will be gradually elevated in the corporate hierarchy.

Most new security managers will come out of colleges and universities. Bachelor and masters degrees may become essential for a successful career. Prior law enforcement, military, and government experience are unlikely to solely qualify a job applicant in the future. Professional status will be required for many security specialties, such as through expanded governmental registration or professional society certification. Certification is likely to be done on the basis of one's area of specialization rather than the contemporary approach which views "security" as a single field. One certification field could be "transportation security specialist."

Security managers and directors will have to understand

computers. Most will have had direct training and experience in computers; many will have some exposure to programming. Those without any experience or training will be lost.

The security guard industry — both contract and proprietary — will develop viable career paths with meaningful opportunities for advancement. Guard salaries will rise far above minimum wage levels. Salaries will be adequate to support a family and security personnel with "roots" will be preferred in hiring. Some post-high school education or training will become increasingly important to being hired as a security guard. Advancement will require at least a two-year (junior college) degree. More will be expected of individual guards than merely walking tours. Greater use will probably be made of "special police status" (Some rights of sworn law enforcement officers) within the jurisdictions the guards serve. Because of continued demands on police departments and their general inability to obtain resources to support these demands, security guards will gradually and increasingly assume many more of the traditional police responsibilities, such as evidenced today by the "Black Sheriffs" private security force guarding the Munich, West Germany subway (underground).

Security directors will probably play a greater role in screening all employees, as well as their own guards. They may also screen non-employees such as independent truck drivers and contractors. The governments (especially in the United States) will gradually loosen restrictions on criminal history background checks of job applications and, to some extent, of all personnel. This will come about as a result of a sense of need and in response to continuing criticism from within and without government.

Courts

Court decisions will continue to place increasingly greater liabilities for losses onto the transportation industry, especially for contract warehouse operations and commercial freight carriers. The courts will demand reasonable care from carriers and warehousing operations. In response to court actions, the insurance industry will place greater demands on security programs in the transportation industry.

Insurance Companies

As noted above, insurance companies will have much more interest in cargo theft and cargo theft statistical information. Meaningful premium reductions will be made available to companies with good security programs. The insurance industry will provide greater and greater support for the development of national and international standards, much as they have done in the past for the fire protection industry.

Life-Safety Conflicts

Building and life-safety codes will eventually play a less dominant role. While life-safety will not be sacrificed in favor of property loss prevention, life-safety requirements which conflict with security considerations will be carefully scrutinized. Realistic trade-offs will be found. Crimes against persons resulting from building designs and construction will be eventually seen to be as important as injuries or deaths of persons caused by fires. Mutually acceptable compromises will be achieved in the design of emergency exit locking systems, such as through the greater use of electro-magnetic locks and time delayed unlocking. The insurance industry's growing interest in security will prompt many of these shifts in emphasis. The transportation industry will benefit from improved perimeter protection capabilities, especially with respect to control over emergency exits.

Standardization

On regional bases, the transportation industry will realize major improvements in efficiency and reliability as standardization in the security field finally sets in. A body of "security standards" will be available for use by national (or regional, such as the European Economic Community) transportation industries; some security standards will be specifically written for transportation. Moreover, cargo documentation will become standardized. This will be especially important for port terminal operations and other locations when multi-carriers are present.

Security equipment will begin to become standardized, especially in specialized areas, such as seals. Transportation security practices will also begin to become much more standardized, although this process will take many more years to become fully realized. Western Europe is currently making much greater progress in security standards development than the United States. There is presently no indication that this gap will soon narrow. The lack of some world-wide standards may prove to be a major new problem area for the transportation security industry.

Transportation Security Associations

In one form or another, national transportation security associations will be formed in most major industrial nations. They will represent all modes, segments, and regions. They are likely to have an international context. The associations will either absorb, replace, or synthesize small, special-interest organizations and associations. The associations will work closely with governments.

Road Transportation

On-the-road cargo theft and truck hijackings will increase over the next fifteen years. Rural areas will see an increase in such crimes as criminals retreat to such locations where less organized small police departments will not have the resources that are available to major city departments. Italy, South America, and portions of Southeast Asia will continue to experience the majority of "armed" hijackings.

More efficient and less expensive electronic "in-cab" logging systems will be available for trucks and vans. These systems will document the history of the vehicle on virtually a minute-by-minute basis. Many drivers will routinely carry alpha-numeric, long-message display pagers. Communications will be two-way between the driver and the central office or dispatcher — possibly on a nation-wide basis.

Electronic intrusion detection and locking systems will be less expensive and will be more reliable. Nation-wide tracking of trucks will be possible at reasonable costs. Such tracking may be made available by service companies on a contract basis. Some satellite tracking systems will emerge, especially for long-haul carriers.

The roads, but especially bridges, will continue to deteriorate and governments will be unwilling to attack the problem until it reaches a crisis level. Truck routes will be shifted and most routes will be increased in time and distance because many bridges will have new weight restrictions. This will be particularly significant for carriers which build larger and heavier vehicles — as is the current trend. The longer routes will also lead to greater cargo loss. Other restrictions may include dedicated truck lanes, dedicated truck roads (more "personal vehicles only" roads), lane segregation, more time-sharing of roads and lanes, more weighing stations, and many more short-haul exclusive truck routes. Less-than-truckload (LTL) restrictions will probably increase. Routes with high cost per ton-mile will be discouraged.

All trucks will have non-removable vehicle indentification markings at multi-points on the vehicle. Nation-wide registration will result in major drops in truck and trailer thefts, as well as of most heavy equipment. More effective governmental programs for tracking stolen vehicles will be developed.

Mass Transit

Major American cities will continue to build mass transit systems. According to Jack Gilstrap, Executive Vice President of the American Public Transit Association (A.P.T.A.), "there is more development going on now than in the past 100 years."[3] There are presently seven major American cities with new rail systems and 13 other mass transit systems are either under construction or are being planned. One reason for this boom is that the United States government is not only providing funds for capital and planning costs, but is picking up 50 percent of operating costs. It is probable, therefore, that the present ridership of about 6.4 percent of American workers will double or triple as the highways become increasingly congested. With this massive influx of riders and systems, the numbers of crime incidents on these systems are bound to increase on the basis of per capita miles by users even if the rate of crime remains the same or even decreases. It is further likely that mass transit police departments will see more resources made available to meet the challenge, especially more personnel. Contract guard services, such as used in Munich's 9.6 mile system, will become increasingly popular. On a world-wide basis, most major "older" systems will upgrade technical security and will increase the size of police forces, much as has been done on London's underground.

The trend away from coin and token fare systems and toward "credit" systems will probably accelerate. Actual credit cards may be developed which would have universal intermodal application within regions, and possibly nationally. These cards could be used for mass transit, and bridge, tunnel, and turnpike tolls. Users would be billed monthly. The use of optical or electronic scanning is possible; such technology would dramatically reduce the "cycle-through" times for users. Fare avoidance crimes will increase significantly in view of the new exposures. The Paris Metro recently estimated that it had about 36 million fare avoidance cases in one year. However, crimes against cash fares will disappear quickly. Criminals will shift their targets to the riders and to the technological vulnerabilities in the system.

Design teams for new mass transit systems will continue the trend toward including security engineers on the team. Environmental design considerations will become prominent in preliminary planning and will aid in reducing crime in coming years.[4]

Water Transportation

Domestic water transportation is unlikely to see major changes, however there may be radical increases in crime on an international scope. Terrorism, political crimes by sovereign states, and piracy directed against fixed and mobil marine assets will continue to grow as major international problems and will significantly effect the security of all marine carriers. Prime targets are likely to be cargo ships, oil platforms (which will be in the multi-thousands by the year 2000), and very high-security marine installations, such as floating nuclear power plants. Long-range global electronic tracking and remote intrusion detection and prevention systems will be developed which will be specifically designed and constructed for these applications. Some systems for some foreign states will include "lethal force" as aspects of security system designs. The Law of the Sea Treaty will see further international cooperation, aspects of which will explicitly address international piracy and related crimes (such as "scuttling" for insurance). Sub-national, national, and international rapid response teams will be created and deployed throughout the world. Increasing numbers of cargo vessels will have on-board response capabilities. Governments will continue to expand their elite "commando" units which will be designated to come to the aid of the merchant ships under attack by pirates or terrorists.

By the year 2000, there will be major increases in the amount of international marine transportation and cargo. Ports and terminal operations will become increasingly difficult to secure due to the volume. Port authority police will see substantial expansion. While port and terminal police operations are presently very labor intensive, in coming years there will be significant increases in the use of electronic security systems. Despite such advances, containerization will be the dominant concept in limiting cargo crime once standardization of operations, equipment (especially reliable seals), and documentation is realized.

Although in-land cargo transport will also see some increases, growth will be limited by congestion of waterways, restrictions on water transport of hazardous materials, and by failures in upgrading and maintaining locks and navigational facilities to keep pace with the growth. The security of locks and navigational facilities will gradually be given priority treatment, but not until the problems reach major proportions. It is possible that private security contract guard firms will begin to play a major role in securing such facilities.

Rail Transportation

Over the next fifteen years, greater emphasis will be given to full automation of the railroad industry, such as by point-to-point computerized electronic tracking of rolling stock and individual shipments. New systems will be developed which refine some earlier attempts which failed, such as remote optical scanning of bar codes on freight and tank cars. Previous technical problems will be overcome. The railroad industry will find more and increased applications for various electronic intrusion detection and access control systems overall.

The failure of rails and railbeds to be adequately upgraded and maintained in some regions of the world (such as the United States, but also others) will gradually lead to routing through fewer and fewer rail lines. This will exacerbate the inevitable increases in congestion on these lines and in the rail yards serving them. Security will become difficult to achieve despite technological advances in systems. Railroad yard police and security forces will be expanded as the need grows, but all railroads will increase the use of contract security guards to meet the demand. As more cargo shifts to the railroad industry, the growth of trailer-on-flat-cars and container- on-flat-cars will lead to increased crime rates as the volume grows, despite security advances.

Air Transportation

In the coming years, air hijackings will continue, but the rate of such incidents will slowly decrease in most nations as countermeasures and programs improve. However, all airports world-wide will see more and tighter security restrictions and controls. Governmental concern about narcotics smuggling on major air carriers today is a harbinger of changes to come. Major new restriction, however, will follow a series of successful armed take-overs of aircraft or hijacking of high-value shipments at some international airports. Some security systems at airports will be readily compromised by the perpetrators, leading to tighter security, after a public outcry.

It is also very probable that sanctions will be eventually imposed on international airports and carriers which do not comply with international airline security standards. The violators are likely to be airlines owned by nation-states.

Pipelines

There will be more than 100,000 miles of pipeline world-wide by the year 2000.[5] Some of the pipelines are critical to various national interests. Because of this, pipelines will see a rapid increase in the use of electronic intrusion detection, surveillance, and alarm assessment technology, some of which will be specifically designed and constructed for pipeline applications. Long-range signal transmission, particularly satellite monitoring, will make these systems viable. Pipelines will be protected by rapid air response teams. Although security forces will continue to be primarily contracted, multinational forces are also likely to be used to strike at saboteurs and for apprehending thieves.

Conclusions

While new problems are certain to emerge along with new solutions, one can feel somewhat optimistic that internation transportation security will realize significant net improvements over the next fifteen years. And while this overview has tended to stress technological advances (because it's far easier to predict), advances will also be made in management theory and practice. International cooperation and organization are also likely to improve and to benefit all nations since, after all, transportation is becoming an increasingly global affair. All in all, people and cargo are likely to move more securely and safely in the coming years. And despite the "ups and downs" one sees year after year, transportation security has been, after all, important to nations for centuries. One has but to recall that one of history's major events, the invasion of the West by the "Golden Horde" of Genghis Khan, was sparked by the "hi-jacking" of a cargo shipment in 1218 in Otrar. However, advances which took centuries to realize, now take decades, and soon will be measured in years!

John J. Strauchs, CPP, Principal of Gage-Babcock & Associates, Inc., a security and fire protection engineering firm, has been Chairman of the National Standing Committee on Transportation Security of the American Society for Industrial Security (A.S.I.S.) since 1979 and is currently on the Board of Directors of the National Cargo Security Council and Chairman of its liaison committee.

1. For a comprehensive overview of the current state-of-the-art and contemporary practices and problems in transportation security, see: Louis A. Tyska and Lawrence J. Fennelly, *Controlling Cargo Theft: A Handbook of Transportation Security,* (Woburn, MA: Butterworth Publication, 1983), 955 pages.
2. For a further discussion of security systems for remote and portable applications, see: John J. Strauchs, "Portable Protection," *Security Management,* Vol. 27, No. 3 (March 1983), pp. 43-47.
3. Susan Tifft, "Mass Transit Makes A Comeback," *Time.* Vol. 123, No. 3 (March 21, 1984), pp. 18-21. Also see *International Security Review,* No. 11 (October, 1980), pp. 56-66.
4. John J. Strauchs, "Security programs Can Miss the Mark," *Controlling Cargo Theft: A Handbook of Transportation Security,* (Woburn, MS: Butterworth Publications, 1983), pp. 663-666. Reprinted from a *Security Management* article, (February 1982).
5. "World Pipeline Plans Total Over 100,000 Miles, $146 Billion," *Pipeline & Gas Journal,* Vol. 209, No. 12 (October 1982), pp. 18-26.

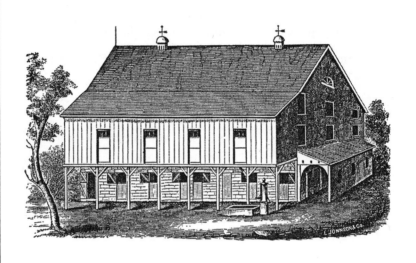

19

Hotel Security in the Year 2000 "A Trip in the Future"

By Hugh Turley

Introduction

The following is a look at how a family will be planning and spending their vacation in the future. Unlike other chapters in this book, it is not the author's intent to be technical. He instead is attempting to present a scenario of future technology which is currently on the drawing boards.

Planning the Vacation

Hugh and Megan Beckley spent at least six months each year and averaged one evening a week during that six months planning, plotting and preparing for their annual vacation. They and their family all agreed that this year's vacation would be at Orlando, Florida and Walt Disney World. They had looked at brochures and magazines and had watched for travel specials throughout each week. The time had come to make the decision on where to go, how long to stay, and what to do.

Financially, Hugh had reached a comfortable level and he had saved enough money this year to afford the very best. Their daughter Devon, who was eight, voted first for Walt Disney World; she and her sister Wendy, who had just turned six, were now old enough to enjoy the wonders of the magic kingdom.

Hugh put in a call to the Buena Vista Palace at "the World" and booked the rooms. He dialed the 800 number to reach reservations for the hotel.

"Good evening," said the computer in a female voice on the other end. "Thank you for calling the Buena Vista Palace at Walt Disney World. Please enter the date you plan to arrive."

Hugh punched in "June 27, 2000," on the phone dialer.

"Thank you, and now punch in the date you wish to check out."

Hugh punched in "July 6, 2000."

"You have selected June 27 to July 6, 2000, for your stay at the Buena Vista Palace. You are confirmed for those dates. Please enter your name."

Hugh punched in the letters of his first name and then last name, wondering if he should have punched his last name first. But there was no comma on the phone.

"Thank you, Mr. Beckley. How many beds will you need?"

He hit the 3 on the phone.

"Three beds," said the lilting computer voice, "one or two rooms?"

He punched 2.

"Two rooms, how many people?"

He punched 4.

"Four," repeated the computer. "If you wish to establish credit at this time for your entire stay, push 1 and then your credit card number. If you wish only to prepay the rooms, push 2 and then your credit card number."

Hugh and his wife had decided to carry as little cash as possible while traveling, so he punched a 1, then his credit card number.

"Your expiration date?"

He punched that in.

"Thank you, Mr. Beckley. Your rooms will be waiting for you. They are now prepaid and debited to your account. In addition, we have established an open account for you in the amount of $1000 which will be charge to your account on June 26th, 2000, as explained in our brochure. Any changes in your plans, please call us back on the same line you dialed to make this reservation. Thank you, again, for selecting the Buena Vista Palace and the staff and management look forward to serving you over the July 4th Holiday. If you need any further assistance, push eight on your phone and an operator will come on the line."

Hugh had no further questions and hung up.

The Beckley family was about to experience the latest in security technology.

Hotel Security of the Future

Hotel room security had come a long way in the past twenty years. The years of the early eighties was the first real thrust in card key systems with hard plastic keys, mylar and cardboard cards that slipped in slots, premade magnetic cards that you took home with you never to be used again, and the hard metal keys with cylinders that were changed periodically at different properties.

But the year 2000 saw the latest in security technology. Hotels had realized that the guests' security and safety had become of primary importance. It was as important as what brand of soap was placed on the sink for an amenity. The enormous awards and great quantity of law suits of the last half of the eighties had made every one in hotel management accept the fact that reasonable and prudent care of the guests had to start with security and looked to the professionals for help and advice.

Security specialists were all in agreement. Whatever the system to help guard and ensure the guests' safety, it should not get in the way of the operation of the establishment. Security directors on the whole followed the concept of setting up perceptual barriers so that would-be thieves would perceive that it was more difficult to target their property than, perhaps, someplace else. Each property took what measures they could afford, but all looked at security as a definite part of doing business. Each tried to anticipate, recognize and appraise any and all risks, and then to initiate some action to remove or reduce those risks. Budgetary considerations were very important, but the savings realized, as compared with the potential losses, were well worth the expense.

At The Hotel

The Beckleys flew into Orlando International Airport and took a limousine to the hotel. When they pulled up to the front of the hotel, they were greeted by a doorman who opened the limo doors, got their luggage out and guided them inside to the front desk for check-in.

"I'll hold your luggage here, sir. Just go over to that open station for check-in procedures."

Hugh went over and sat at the computer terminal. A lady in a bright uniform was there to help him.

"Welcome to the Buena Vista Palace, sir. Would you like me to fill in the information for you or would you like to do it yourself?"

Most people let the lady fill in the information because they were on vacation, however some people just liked doing it themselves. Besides, it was so much easier than the old days.

"No, I'd like to do it myself, thank you."

Hugh inserted his credit card in the slot indicated. The screen immediately was filled with all his reservation information.

"Your reservation shows you arriving today and leaving on July 6. Is that still the same, Mr. Beckley?" asked the lady.

"Yes."

"Fine. It shows you have a credit of $1000 for all your incidentals, food, lounge, game room, et cetera, while you are on the property. How many people will be needing keys."

"All four of us, I guess . . . however, the kids will be in a connecting room so I'd like us all to have keys for each room."

"Well, how about if we set it up so you have the same for both rooms?"

"Okay."

"Very well, sir. Here is how it works. This is the very latest state-of-the-art in key operations. See that plate there? Just lay your hand on the plate and press this button."

Hugh put his right hand down flat on the glass and a light swept under the glass as if it were a copy machine as soon as he pushed he button.

"Now, if each of your party will do the same. You see, your palm print is your key. I had entered the fact that you want room 2625 and 2626 equal for all four people to be able to enter."

"When you get to your room, you will merely place your hand on the reader beside the door and as it reads your hand, it will unlock the door. The door will stay unlocked for four seconds and then relock itself."

Wendy could barely reach the light so they decided not to have her do it because they didn't usually give her a key anyway.

Devon thought is was neat and Megan found it fascinating, like a scene from a movie.

The lady pressed another button and the folio for all charges, credits and information were printed out. She handed it to Hugh.

"While here on your vacation, if you wish to charge anything throughout the hotel, merely place your hand on the screen at each cashier's station and it will automatically encode it to your account. This way no one else can use your credit, for only you have your palm print. Your entire family, except the little one, can charge also unless you wish to limit it."

Hugh figured he should limit Devon as she may not totally understand the limits of credit. So he did.

"The system is set up from a computer to all the rooms in the hotel. As you have pressed your hand on the screen, it read your prints, recorded them, passed them through fiber optics to your designated rooms and made it possible to offer you the finest form of security possible in the hotel industry. I hope you and your family enjoy each moment here."

Hugh and his wife wondered what could they possibly think of next? Perhaps your voice? Imagine walking up to your door and saying your name and the door opens.

Anything is possible with today's computer, lasers, fiber optics, copying techniques, etc. The possibilities are only limited by man's imagination.

20

Residential Security in the Year 2000

by Michael S. Kaye, President

Westec Security, Inc.

In 1983, a study made by California home builders revealed that residential security had become the second greatest concern among those families purchasing new homes. Ranked number one by new home buyers was locations of the residence in relation to schools and employment.

What those builders discovered was that, at least in California, and there is no reason to believe it is any different in most large urban areas in the United States, residential security systems are becoming as common in American homes as microwave ovens.

The reason for this phenomena can be easily understood when a 1985 report from the U.S. Department of Justice shows that almost a million people are at home each year when a burglar breaks-in, and about a third fall victim to a violent crime, including rape and assault.

According to the department's Bureau of Justice Statistics, 13 percent of 73 million burglaries that occurred from 1973 through 1982 found someone at home at the time of the break-in. In other words, almost 9.5 million people were surprised by burglars during the ten-year period.

Steven Schlesinger, the bureau director, was quoted by United Press International as saying, "Household burglary ranks among the more serious felony crimes because a substantial proportion of the violent crimes that occur in the home take place during a burglary. Burglary is a potentially far more serious crime than its classification as a property offense indicates," he said.

Is it any wonder then, that Americans are no spending more than 45 billion each year on alarm systems and services.

This certainly confirms a study made by J.P. Freeman of Newtown, Conn., about which the Wall Street Journal reported in October 1984. The study found that in 1978, one in 83 households had a professionally installed residential alarm system. That figure is presently one in 11, and by the year 1990, it is predicted that one in four households will own a system.

The expenditures for private security programs, goods and services exceed the combined total of local, state and federal law enforcement expenditures. Overall, in The Hallcrest Report, published by Chancellor Press in 1985, it was noted that more than $20 billion is spent each year for private protection provided by a labor force of 1.1 million employees in various facets of private security in the United States.

An interesting footnote to these statistics is the fact that both English and American policing have roots in private protection initiatives.

The legal basis for the right to protect one's property in this country derives from English common law tradition and the right to engage others to protect property. This has been established under the Constitution. Some states have enacted specific statutes which allow individuals to protect themselves, their property and their right to employ third parties to exercise those rights on their behalf.

It is well to understand, however, that the authority of private security personnel is usually the same as that of a private citizen in making arrests. In other words, a person employed as a security officer can only make a "citizen's arrest."

Going back to the historical nature of private security,

landowners in 18th century England employed armed gamekeepers to protect their property. As society grew and became more complex, public protection with paid police began replacing private protection. In England, the early efforts of tythingmen, watchmen, constables, sheriffs and special police units were directed primarily toward maintaining order in a growing society.

In the mid-1800's, watchmen, beltmen and door "rattlers," were replaced by organized police departments in the United States.

In 1829, during the beginning of organized police protection, the founder of the famous London "Bobbies," Sir Robert Peel, explained to the people, "We're forming a body of men who will be paid to do what every citizen has a moral and legal obligation to do for themselves."

By 1853, a Somerville, Maine man, Augustus Pope, had patented one of the first electric burglar alarm systems.

It was developed with electro-magnetic contacts which were mounted on doors and windows and wired to a a battery and bell. Pope sold his invention to Edwin Holmes who took the system to New York City where he sold the first alarms to wealthy homeowners.

He also used electrified metal foil and screens which are still widely used today by many alarm companies. In addition, he built the first central communications center where bank and jewelry vaults were connected by wire so that they could be monitored in a central station.

By the 1870's and '80's, large mansions and businesses were being protected against fire with heat sensors. William Watkins of New York City was the first to use these sensors in a central monitoring station and formed the company known today as AFA Protective.

The use of these systems began to spread. In Chicago, a district telegraph company was providing protection against fire via a central station. Before long, other companies were marketing both fire and burglar alarm systems.

In 1901, these local companies were consolidated by Western Union into the American District Telegraph Company which is known today as ADT.

Since that time, thousands of alarm companies have entered the field. The National Burglar & Fire Alarm Association estimates that over 12,000 companies are engaged in the residential security and fire alarm business.

Competition and innovation in the alarm industry have made protection more available to middle income families — that and the harsh reality that crime exists everywhere, in the inner city, the suburbs and everywhere in-between.

Our company is a perfect example of what began to happen in the late 1960's as a result of the rising fear of crime across the country. Westec Security, Inc., had its origins as Westinghouse Security Systems, Inc., a subsidiary of Westinghouse Electric. It was formed in 1968 to design and market security systems for the home.

Westinghouse had purchased a small Minneapolis company which had developed some very imaginative concepts for residential security and these included: the first digital dialers for telephone transmission; the first alarm activation talk-in device; the first prestigious sophisticated home demonstrator; and, the novel sales concept (for the alarm industry) of out-right sale of the product and the system.

In 1979, Westinghouse decided to concentrate on other areas and discontinue marketing consumer products. As the largest and most successful dealer of Westinghouse security systems, Westec purchased the security division from Westinghouse.

This was a period of rapid growth throughout the industry. By November 1982, Westec was acquired by Secom Ltd., the largest security company in Japan. Westec's manufacturing operations were moved to Orange County, California and became not only the largest manufacturer of home security systems, but also one of the largest companies to have direct sales and installation experience.

This experience resulted in the development of a product line and services specifically designed to meet the needs of the consumer in the home. Heretofore, most residential installations were adaptations of those used in commercial applications.

During the early formative years of the company, there

were many problems pioneering in the marketplace. Originally, when our salespersons would call offering Westinghouse Security, they would often get the reply, "No thank you, we do our business with Merrill Lynch!"

The market is now fully aware of residential security companies like Westec.

As pointed out, previously, competition and innovation in the industry have made residential security more affordable. Although, many people in Southern California think of residential security as something that is available for the rich and very rich, our Westec yard signs can be seen not only in the very affluent neighborhoods of Beverly Hills, Bel Air, Palos Verdes and La Jolla, but our blue sign has become even more visible in middle-income sections of the vast Souther California suburbia.

The reason for this is that over the past few years, technological innovations have increased the availability of home security systems.

Although the basic concept remains the same — a sensor of some type, detects an emergency and signals for assistance, today's equipment is more reliable because of the new technology in electronics.

Computers, printed circuits, digital communicators, and microprocessors have refined monitoring and signaling technology, and modern electronic sensors now include ultrasonic, infrared and microwave devices which were formerly available only in more sophisticated commercial and industrial applications.

Indeed, the systems available today can be personalized to offer maximum protection wherever they are installed. In 1985, Westec introduced its W-3000, a unit so sophisticated that is has a voice of its own which instructs the client in the use of the system.

In addition, such variables as the size, construction and accessibility of the home, lifestyle patterns, presence of children and pets, domestic duties and contents value are all weighted in the tailoring of a workable residential system.

Today's systems come complete with many devices to provide protection in the home. They offer multiple levels of home security, depending upon the needs of the client. Systems can be provided for everything from a single condominium with only two entrances — to an entire gated community where thousands of sensors are independently supervised by an on site computerized central station. Westec and its competitors do this in many communities.

Back in 1981, Westec introduced a system that included receiving and monitoring equipment capable of supervising every individual sensor of each system and sensing trouble or tampering, from an actual unauthorized entry. The equipment was solid-state and designed by Westec to support cable TV multiplex applications, either alone or with telephone redundancy.

The features that were introduced in 1981 became standard on most systems. These included:

Alarm Memory - The system's Central Access Terminal (CAT) displays the point of any attempted intrusion on the MST control panel screen.

Duress Control - Provices alarm protection in the home or yard against an intruder.

Direct Voice Command - Allows voice communication directly to the communicaitons center during an emergency.

Zone Display - Shows the status of every protected area in the home via the CAT.

Door Guardian - Especially important for homes with small children and swimming pools.

Visual Alarm Status - No guessing about fire, burglary or medical emergency. Alarm information is transmitted to the communications center where required assistance is expedited.

Special - The home or individual room's temperature can be monitored to prevent damage to frozen pipes or summer temperatures.

Select-A-Code - Provides entry for maid or serviceman.

Continuous State Circuit Analyzers - Monitors all sensor circuits automatically to detect malfunctions. Helps reduce false alarms.

There are, of course, many other components in a home security system, such as: sensing devices; mechanical contact switches, mercury-flow switches, a device similar to a level which is used on doors and windows that tilt open; pressure switches, used under mats and rug; custom-made alarm screens; invisible light beams, ultrasonic detectors; radar detectors; microwave detectors; vibration detectors; and heat detectors.

Depending upon how elaborate a system is desired and the homeowner's budget, there are many more sophisticated devices that can be used today.

An owner of a large estate may opt for closed-circuit television, strategically placed microphones that can be monitored at the central station to pick up intrusion sounds, such as attempts to climb a wall.

If one is concerned about people calling at the front door, an eye scanner can be installed that reads and matches the back of the retina before allowing access. There are also photo- alarms which take Polaroid pictures of an intruder every six seconds and video tape machines that are activated in a similar fashion.

One new device is a garage door opener that automatically bolts the lower edges of the door upon closing. A homeowner may also install a more sophisticated system that scrambles the normal layout of the numeric keypad. It is designed, also, so that the numbers become illegible to anyone other than the authorized person.

What does this portend for the future? Although the Justice Department has noted a slight decrease in the amount of crime in urban areas, the figures do not give an adequate picture of what has happened in the suburbs. There has been a shift that has seen more women venturing out into the work force, leaving the home vacant during the day.

Almost 70 percent of all residential burglaries take place duing the day when no one is at home or around to hear, see or deter the intruder.

In 1983, Time Magazine said America had created a bunker mentality that has turned the country into a fortressed society.

Last year (1985) a detective in the West Los Angeles Police Department told the Los Angeles Times, in a feature story on crime, a very interesting story. He said that after apprehending

two persons in the Pacific Palisades area who were responsible for 40 burglaries, the pair admitted that they hit only
homes that didn't have security company signs on their front
lawns.

It means that even the estimate we noted earlier of an
alarm system being installed in every one out of five homes
by the year 1990 is probably low. The year 2000 is only 14
years away as this is being written. What will happen in
residential security is anyone's guess. However, the day you
could go out for the afternoon and leave your doors unlocked
with no fear that your home would be entered, or you could
leave your keys in the car with no fear that it would be gone
is long past.

The future offers some hope in deterring the breaking and
entering of private property. The technology of fiber optics
should provide a revolutionary approach to alarm systems.

Optical fibers have no metallic content or electric current
and thus can independently transmit individual sensor outputs.

Alarm systems using this method are not susceptible to
electrical interference and signal interception or distortion
and will reduce false alarsm.

Almost all systems today are hooked up to a central station
via the telephone lines. In addition, many systems are adding
radio transmitters as backup. However, as the promise of
fully integrated systems through advancements in microprocessors, computers, fiber optics and microwave improve,
there is every reason to believe that emergency informatin
could be provided by satellite data transmission that will have
a profound effect on the way emergency situations are now
handled.

Think of it, electronic signaling via push buttons could
become obsolete. A voice activated password could open
your garage door. Your house could become completely key-
less. A magnetic card such as used for your automatic teller
machine at the bank would open the front door. Here again,
voice activation could be used, or the front door would open
only when a family member pressed their thumb against a
screen. An optical readout would identify the thumb print and
open the door. Once inside tiny hidden microprocessors cap-

able of artificial intelligence would constantly identify you and your family and automatically reset the alarm system. You would, however, be able to go anywhere in the house without setting off a false alarm.

These are only a few of the changes we foresee as we gaze into our crystal ball to the year 2000 and beyond.

Acknowledgements - Much of the background information for this chapter was obtained from the following sources: National Burglar & Fire Alarm Association; The Hallcrest Report: Private Security and Police in America, William C. Cumnningham and Todd H. Taylor, Chancellor Press, 1985; The Wall Street Journal; The Los Angeles Times; Building Industry Association of California; U. S. Department of Justice; Time Magazine.

21

Sporting Event Security in the Year 2000

Joe Shirley, CCP

Director Corporate Security

Turner Broadcasting

"The four pillars of government . . . religion, justice, counsel and treasure."
FRANCIS BACON

In the past decade, crowd control has become a major concern of everyone associated with sports. The problems continue to increase at an alarming rate with injuries, game disruptions, vandalism, and even fatalities.

Crowd control today Is a phenomenon so new that there are no textbooks on the subject. However, after twenty years of experience in crowd control, ranging from riots in Central America to stadiums with 80,000 rock fans, I have been able to document the changes and to consider the possibilities of the future.

In order to consider these new methods, one must first reflect on incidents of the past few years. The degrees of violence have varied with possibly the worse yet to come. The following incidents illustrate the recent negative trends in crowd behavior:

1. Eleven were killed in a panic at a rock concert.
2. A security officer was thrown head first over the rail by football fans.
3. A riot occurred in a stadium after a rock group failed to perform in the rain. Many policemen and spectators were injured.

4. A fan ran onto the playing field with a knife in hand.
5. Sniper fire wounded three people during a high school football game.
6. Fans stormed the stage at a concert causing injuries to police and security officers.
7. At least 600 people were injured at a stadium concert.
8. Many professional baseball players have been hit by hard objects thrown from the stands.
9. A concert crowd so damaged a playing field that a professional baseball game was cancelled a week later.
10. During a New England Patriot's game, fifty male fans urinated onto a crowd sitting below.
11. In 1976, a fan had a heart attack while viewing a professional football game. While aid was being given, another fan urinated on the medical staff and the victim.
12. During the famous Cleveland Beer Riot, three security officers were thrown over an upper deck railing.
13. On December 9, 1974, fighting fans, unhappy with a referee's decision, rioted in Madison Square Gardens. They not only tore out seats and ceiling panels, but they also set part of the arena on fire.
14. In 1964, 300 spectators were killed in a brawl after a disputed call in a soccer match in Lima, Peru.
15. Guatemalan fans once attacked a soccer team with machetes, hacking five player to death.
16. After three World Cup Soccer matches between El Salvador and Honduras ignited riots in 1969, the two countries severed diplomatic relations and eventually went to war.
17. According to a Soviet newspaper, a Moscow scientific worker was so drunk when he left a football match that upon seeing a trolley bus without a crew, he drove it home. The newspaper listed that incident as representative of a deterioration of the behavior of Soviet sports fans.

18. In Tel Aviv, Israel, fans stormed the field near the end of a soccer match and an Israeli soccer player was stabbed to death.

If the current trend of violence continues, improvements in the established methods of crowd control will be greatly needed. Various techniques have proved to be successful. While some should suffice for the next few years, others will soon be outdated by the need for futuristic automation. The areas we have to consider will not only be the sporting event itself, but also the time period before and after the event. Most definitely to be considered will be security activities occurring near parking lots, the tickets windows, stadium gates, and inside the facility.

Parking Lot Security

When one thinks of crowd control at sporting events, the efficiency must begin at the first point of contact — the parking lot.

As more spectators arrive earlier for tailgating parties, the possibilities for criminal incidents become even greater. Within the vast areas of parking, crimes on the rise include auto thefts, rapes, robberies, ticket scalping, assaults, and even murder. Since good parking lot security has a profound influence on fans prior to entering the stadium, diverse techniques are essential. Observation, lighting, and communication are the major concerns.

Security observation of such large areas can best be handled through the use of helicopters, mounted horse patrols, and motorized golf carts. Whereas helicopters provide wide angled observation with available large search lights, the mounted patrol enables the officer to see over the cars and respond quickly. In addition, motorized golf carts supply quick response to smaller, hard to reach areas while stationary cameras and observation towers focus on hard to view areas.

To alleviate possible problems of parking lot security in the year 2000, major changes are already being made within the areas of mass transit. Rapid transit systems using computerized trains and people movers will be necessary to accomodate the large numbers attending sporting events and to aid in the elimination of congested parking facilities.

However, since many fans will still prefer to drive personal vehicles, changes in parking lot security must be met using a minimal amount of manpower. The entrance to parking facilities will no longer be manned by people handling parking fees. Instead, computerized machines will receive the money and make the necessary change. As the drivers proceed through the parking lot, computerized machinery will direct the driver to a designated space. Proper surveillance of such vast facilities can only be successfully achieved through the use of mounted cameras freely moving on cables stretched above all areas. In addition, the sophisticated "eyes" will include night vision, zoom lense, and a public announcement system. Fine tuning devices will also enable any unusual sounds to be detected so that quick response can be made if a person is in distress.

Whereas crime increases during night hours, lighting devices will be engineered to remain on until all movement has ceased and to reactivate when activity resumes. This will insure the safety of all post game departures.

Ticket Window Sales

In a society where the mottoes "Win At Any Cost" and "First Is Best" are becoming more prevalent in our everyday actions, situations of pressure can lead to dangerous problems at ticket windows.

As it is not uncommon for fans to gather at these windows up to 48 hours or more prior to the designated time of sales, problems of sanitation, pickpockets, placement in line, and general panic are becoming growing concerns. Sanitation facilities must be suitably provided and medical aid available to handle any emergency.

Currently, security officers patrolling these areas can successfully create a buffer zone between the ticket windows and the buyers. By placing crowd control stands or saw horses around the buffer zone, a possible general panic caused by pushing and shoving can be avoided. Once the

50-75 feet buffer zone is created, security personnel can establish and maintain lines for approaching the ticket windows. A second buffer zone is often necessary in the event of thousands of early ticket buyers. For safety reasons, fixed barriers or crowd control lanes made of metal are not recommended for large crowds.

Once again, as the years progress, computerized automation will be necessary to provide the most convenient means of ticket sales. As the fan approaches the ticket window, available seating will be listed on a computerized screen. After the customer has selected and paid for requested seats, the computer will dispense the tickets.

Security of these automatic tellers will be monitored from a central station. Customer lines will also be under surveillance by microphones and cameras so that in the event of a customer robbery, the sales area will automatically be secured and the perpetrator trapped. Response will then be made by security officers from the central station.

Gate Security

Inadequate security at stadium gates can result in a variety of problems. If fans shove against turnstiles, crash gates, smuggle in bottles, cans, or alcoholic beverages, or panic in an emergency exiting procedure, unnecessary injuries could occur. Thus, in order to insure good traffic flow and ease the tension by fans, it is advisable to always open more gates than one thinks is necessary.

Efficient ticket takers, uniformed security personnel, clearly stated policies on posted signs, and gates in good working order are all matters to be considered currently when handling gate security.

However, with the dawning of the year 2000, technology advances will be utilized to provide efficient, safe flow of all fans entering and exiting sporting events. Turnstiles will soon accept tickets while a security officer supervises the passage of fans through a metal detector in order to check for weapons and explosives. To prevent projectiles from being thrown into the gate areas, wire mesh gate construction will soon be replaced by a solid material. These mechanically controlled gates will be encased with emergency lighting, panic bars, P.A. systems, cameras, and automatic locking devices.

Inside The Stadium

Once the fans are inside the stadium, a crowd control plan has to take on many facets. It is essential that a facility housing fifty to a hundred thousand fans has a large, well trained, uniformed security force. This can consist of police as well as in-house or contract security personnel. The uniformed staff should be physically fit and well trained in the mechanics of arrest and handling violent individuals in crowds. Additionally, they should carry handcuffs, a baton, and mace. Much emphasis should be placed on the public relations aspect as well. It is a proven fact that a well trained, uniformed security person who is courteous and helpful will encourage fans to visit the facility again.

Techniques used in other parts of the stadium will also be instrumental inside the stadium. In addition, procedures incorporating video taping of unruly spectators, emergency lighting, and emergency evacuation should already be in practice.

As one approaches the future and new crowd control manuals are written, causes of our current trends in sports violence must be understood. It is necessary to realize that all crowds contain the ingredients for violence. The sports fan of the future will engage in more violent activities that could influence the outcome of the game. Raw emotions surface in individuals during a crowded situation where one often feels a mask of anonymity is worn. Instead of feeling responsible for one's own actions, the blame is often put on the responsibility of the crowd. The result can be unusual, impromptu violence.

Through satellite communications, fans will be exposed more to international events in the sports world as well as the political world. This increase in interest will bring more fans to sporting events. As seen in the Olympic Games of 1976, the sports arena can become a political arena as well, if televised on an international scale.

Where else can terrorism find a mass gathering of people who will permit them easy escape? Even though advanced technology can control many aspects of security in crowd control, can human contact be fully eliminated from a society of emotions?

A special thank you is given to Gail Prichard and Karen Lowden of Turner Broadcasting for their help with this chapter.

22

Retail Security in the Year 2000

Peter H. Jones, F.I.P.I., F.I.I. SEC.

M.B.I.M

London, England

*"The theory of Communism may be summed up in one sentence:
Abolish all private property."*
KARL MARX & FRIEDRICH ENGELS

Whilst security practitioners are usually concerned solely with current facts, are not generally accustomed to gazing into crystal balls in order to project the future, in doing so on this occasion they must take a fairly optimistic and realistic view of their projections; however, some brief fleeting mention must be given to the views of the vociferous minority who, in pessimistic fashion, express politically motivated doubts on whether or not this planet Earth, or indeed the whole universe, will in fact exist in the year 2000.

In casting aside the forecasts of the prophets of doom and despondency and taking a rather more cheerful and practical approach to the future, one must accept that retail security in the year 2000 will depend entirely, as it does now, on the demands made by the lifeblood of any retail organisation - the customer - the fickle individual whose extensive and unusual demands must be satisfied.

What changes in social patterns are going to dictate the requirements of the customer? Life style shows every indication of substantial change and current newsworthy events tend to point towards such questionable progress as the working week being shorter, possibly 4 days, retail premises probably being open for business for 7 days per week and with longer daily opening hours.

These two factors will create a two edged situation. Customers, that is the general public, will have far more leisure time through either earlier retirement or less commitment to work. This will put pressure on them to buy with their guaranteed incomes a wider range of living and leisure merchandise. On an internal basis, retailers will find it necessary to employ a greater numerical staff, all-be-it some of the part-time, because of the shorter working week and to cope with the longer opening hours. The personnel and training functions will be extended to ensure that the right staff are recruited and that they are all appropriately trained to serve the customer to a very high standard; certainly a higher standard than experienced at present. Training could well be considered as a statutory requirement.

It is probable that the life style of customers will be such that they will be less tolerant of imperfections in either merchandise or service and the only retailer capable of progression, or indeed remaining in business, will be the retailer who has the ability to "get the whole package right."

The older type of multi-floored department or chain store will be a thing of the past, probably pulled down or used for other purposes. The modern retail outlet will be a two floored compact structure, purpose built, within a city centre precinct or a specially constructed retail connurbation located out of town but within easy commuting for customers. Stores will be all purpose built. The most successful will be those which have been planned in considerable detail in respect to the facilities and merchandise it is intended they should provide. There will be minimal layout flexibility.

Of course, progress in technology will be a major influence on the retail sector of business. Point of sale equipment will be further refined and miniaturised and the cashless society with its attendant and well publicised security problems will be a reality.

The personal selection of goods by customers on the shop floor will be substantially reduced as the acquisition of relatively standard items will be carried out via orders placed by use of television sales procedures reaching nearly every home and payment made through pre-arranged credit facilities.

Overall, technological progress will be principally electronic with the micro-chip and micro-processor playing an even greater role than it does at present.

With the adjustments to trading patterns caused by customers' attitudes and fluctuating but progressive corporate facilities, a complete re-assessment by retailers of their loss control principles will be necessary. What sort of loss will be tolerated. Will that loss be expressed, as it is now as a percentage of turnover, or will it be expressed as a percentage of profit? Probably, to bring loss rates into a proper perspective, the latter will be more likely and of far more real significance and interest to shareholders who will be primarily interested in the generation of additional personal income.

Those responsible for the creation of legislation will be extremely active over the coming years as a result of pressure from minority groups seeking to further their own beliefs and, indeed, rights, irrespective of the beliefs and rights of others. As a result of this, Courts of Law will be inundated with pleas of "not guilty" and many of those appearing as defendants before such Courts will be found "not guilty" simply on technical grounds or conflicting legislation and semi-official but generally acceptable codes of practice.

The application of security or loss control measures will have to be very clearly defined and positively enforced.

Although the general level of security staffing in retail establishments will be similar to today, the calibre of personnel involved will be much higher, far more retail management orientated. The actual Job Descriptions will be substantially upgraded. The days of second career security operatives will be long gone and career prospects will have to be offered to direct entry specialist security employees. Professional security associations and institutions will play a far greater and wider role in personal and general security education in retail communities. Specialist security operatives will be expected to assume a position professionally relative to the professional appointments which they will occupy.

It is unlikely that the cost of crime will be any less than it is today, taking into consideration the normal inflationary factors. However, the overall pattern of crime in a retail environment will be very different. Gone will be the days of theft of merchandise of relatively low financial value. There will, of course, still be the odd such incident, but the trend will be towards fewer crimes numerically with each individual offense being of substantial value.

Rather than merchandise orientated crime, the general tendency will be in the direction of paperwork or computer generated irregularities resulting in the diversion of substantial sums of money through indirect cash transfer.

There will be a distinct social division of offenders between the "have's" and the "have not's" within society. Whilst those who "have" firstly a job of gainful employment and secondly a reasonable standard of living, will be reluctant to jeopardise their privileged position for relatively little financial gain, some will do so. The "have not's" will strive to achieve a similar standard of living without the necessity of working in the standard and acceptable way to reach that position. Unemployment will continue to present a problem to a progressive and consumer orientated society.

The "have's" will therefore be responsible for high value crime as a result of accessibility to it and must be projected to join the ranks of the "have not's" when caught. The "have not's," being responsible for what could be considered as petty crime, will care little about their predicament or the consequences of being caught offending. They will increasingly rely on the State for their continued will-being...and indeed, for a standard of living which is raised at a rate which far outweighs their overall financial value to society.

In-house protection of stock will continue to use the principles of electronic article surveillance, closed circuit television and two-way radio communication. But a strong liklyhood exists that physical protection in the form of locks, bolts and bars, etc., will be far more dominant than it is in the 1980's.

Article surveillance tags will serve a dual purpose to their present primary function. They will also bear pure merchandising information such as stock codes and selling prices.

Systems will be more extensively used.

By the year 2000, closed circuit television within retail outlets, probably linked with a two-way sound facility, will be far more widespread and flexible, in colour and accepted as being an effective tool of management in fields other than pure security. Fibre optics will be considered as the normal means of picture communication.

Security application generally will be on a total loss control basis.

Price differentials between the High Street giants and the single unit retailer will be far more pronounced than at present, the latter being utilised by customers mainly on a principle of convenience shopping for which an extra price will have to be paid.

Valuable merchandise will be retailed on a principle of seeing but not touching. Initial interest will be generated purely on sight with controlled handling facilities for those whose interest in purchasing goes one step further.

Cut-throat competition will exist between retailers striving to satisfy an ever less tolerant community of customers. Security or loss control will be one of the few areas where operational necessity will dictate co-operation rather than competition. Flat packs for hard merchandise will be the order of the day as space savers in respect to storage, and customers will be expected to carry these away themselves after purchase. Delivery charges will be the alternative, but delivery of any merchandise will be anticipated on a next day principle.

What can be projected as an acceptable loss rate? With profit margins cut to maintain a competitive place in the battle of the High Streets, every retailer will be striving to keep losses at the lowest possible level. Those whose losses exceed 1% of turnover will be hard pushed to remain in business.

One thing stands out. Full cognisance will have to be taken by management of loss control on a basis of the widest possible meaning of the expression. Those who fail to assess fully and react appropriately will stand every chance of not surviving.

Trend Setting for the Future

We will see the day when people will be sitting at home in front of their television computer doing their weekly food shopping. A twist of the knob, a flick of the dial and your shopping is done. Computers will play a big part in the supermarket and retail business - from automated weighing machines to electronic checkout scanners. In Los Angeles, California, at a store called *Phone In - Drive Thru* allows customers to call in orders to a computer operator. The customer then drives to the pick-up place, pays the bill plus a small service charge, and shopping is completed. In Japan computers and robots are doing the same type of shopping for customers.

The overall conclusion must be that only the fittest will survive the turn of the century.

23

The Guard in the Year 2000

Randolph D. Brock III, CPP

"Common sense is instinct. Enough of it is genius."
GEORGE BERNARD SHAW

Unlike technologies not yet conceived, the human guard who will be on duty in the year 2000 is alive today. To the extent that the guard force in the year 2000 is composed of persons aged 35 or above, the basic educational level has already been determined and the guard has lived through his or her formative years, the years which will go far to shape the attitudes and perspectives which the guard will bring to the job. Thus, to some extent in dealing with the human component of security in the year 2000, a portion of that future is now part of history.

The last 15 years has witnessed continuing evolution of the guarding function from the watchman of the 19th century to the security officer of the late 20th. Some of the more significant and observable changes have included:

- A dramatic increase in the number of women in security officer positions.
- A reduction in the average age of security guards.
- An increase in the average educational level of contract security guards.
- Increased regulation of guards at the state level, both in terms of screening and mandatory training.

- An increase in numbers of both contract and proprietary security guards, at a rate of increase significantly
outstripping that of public law enforcement.

Although there has been change, some of it important,
many things have not changed materially. Uniforms continue
to look much as they did in the past, despite a trend in some
locations towards the soft, or "blazer-type," uniform. Guards
have continued to make "rounds" or patrols of industrial
plants, to perform checks of identification at access control
points, to respond to incidents, and to otherwise continue
with the traditional role as protectors of people, property and,
increasingly, of information. The tools which guards employed
changed relatively little during the last 15 years, despite a
continuing increase in reliance upon electronic aids, such as
closed circuit television and alarm annunciators.

In theory the increase in the sophistication of electronic
monitoring devices should have decreased the need for the
human element. To some extent this has been the case; but,
this decrease has been overshadowed by the dramatic increase in the total number of security guards employed.

In other words, notwithstanding the technological advances
which have provided electronic and mechanical means of
performing tasks which in past years would have required
human intervention, something else was occurring which
caused a net increase in the number of guards used. That
something else was the perception that a visible security
presence was needed to deal with a perceived, and sometimes very real and growing threat.

Fear of crime has been the single greatest impetus to the
growth of numbers of guards. Who would have thought 15
years ago that virtually every small boutique in midtown
Manhattan would employ one or more uniform security
guards?

Secondary factors include the growth of forms of business
which are often dependent upon the uniformed security guard
as a primary means of protection, such as suburban shopping
malls and inner city fast food restaurants. Additionally, the
trend, though still relatively small, of privatization — the assumption by the private sector of security roles traditionally

reserved for government — has added to the numbers of guards currently employed, particularly by the federal government. Had it not been for legislative intervention, principally at the behest of public employee unions, this trend would have been even more significant.

GUARDS IN SOME COMPANIES WILL CONTINUE TO EXIST, EVEN IF THEY CAN BE REPLACED BY TECHNOLOGY, BECAUSE THE CHAIRMAN OF THE BOARD DOES NOT WANT TO BE GREETED BY A ROBOT.

Guards are clearly the most expensive component in the security equation, and their use now is typically limited to those situations which require human intervention, discriminating judgment or some other uniquely human quality that technology has yet to be able to supplant. However, there is nevertheless the psychological or emotional reason which causes guards to be employed as a solution. Foremost among them is the concept, often strong in many corporation and/or organizational cultures, that mechanical security means, particularly employed as access and egress points, is somehow dehumanizing or contrary to the kind of image the organization wishes to project. Although such feelings can be expected to lessen as technology becomes more pervasive, the year 2000 will still see the guard in his or her traditional role in this regard. Secondarily, fear of crime, rather than crime itself, will continue to fuel guard force expansion.

GUARDS WILL BE REDUCED IN NUMBER IN MANY ORGANIZATIONS BECAUSE THEIR SPIRALLING COST CANNOT BE JUSTIFIED IN THE FACE OF TECHNOLOGIES WHICH CAN ACCOMPLISH THE SAME FUNCTIONS. THE GROWTH OF THE CONTRACT GUARD INDUSTRY WILL SLOW, AS COSTS FOR MANPOWER RISE AND COSTS FOR TECHNOLOGIES FALL.

No security director or contract security manager has not seen in the past five years a continuing erosion in the number of guard posts at larger facilities as technology is used to replace guard manpower. The development of increasingly sophisticated electronic tools can be expected to continue the relentless reduction of costly manpower, particularly as the cost for electronics, as expected, continues to decline.

The result will be a lowering in the growth projection for guard expansion as we move toward the year 2000. Projections by the Bureau of Labor Statistics shows that slowing of growth rate to have already begun.

THE CONTRACT GUARD INDUSTRY WILL BE SUBJECTED TO INCREASINGLY ONEROUS REGULATION BECAUSE OF ITS INABILITY OR UNWILLINGNESS TO LOBBY EFFECTIVELY FOR MEANINGFUL REFORM AND CONTROL.

Each news story exposing significant or widespread misconduct by guards can be expected to continue the trend of tightening regulation to prevent entry into the occupation of those with criminal records. In recent years, several states have adopted legislation mandating preassignment training, weapons qualification, criminal history searches and similar stratagems designed to weed out convicted felons and to prevent some of the worst abuses, particularly in the area of shootings, by guards. Legislative attempts are ongoing in several jurisdictions to mandate that criminal record checks be completed prior to guards being employed. Statistics, such as those offered by New York, to the effect that one in ten contract guards (in some cases as many as one in four) have criminal records, have added impetus to this movement. Attempts by various organizations within the contract guard industry to introduce so-called model licensing and regulation bills have been sporadic, fragmented and generally unsuccessful.

Over the next 15 years increasing clamor to regulate the contract guard industry can be expected. In at least several key states the likelihood is strong that prehire criminal record checks as well as mandatory preassignment training for contract guards will be in effect by the year 2000. This is something the industry will learn to live with and, after some adjustment, these requirements will not severely impede the delivery of services.

It is equally likely that the proprietary guard forces in most of these jurisdictions will escape this kind of regulation, principally because of their stronger political clout. Although at first blush, there would be a tendency to assume that proprietary security forces would thus obtain a "competitive" advantage over contract, cost considerations as well as the contract industry's ability to adapt to these new constraints, will not seriously affect the continued conversion from proprietary to contract in many industries.

It is most likely that spiralling civil lawsuit awards, coupled with the high cost of liability insurance, will provide a greater impetus for improving training and selection than all the new regulations and mandatory training combined.

CONTRACT GUARDS WILL BE INCREASINGLY DIRECTED BY PROPRIETARY SUPERVISORS. THE TREND TOWARD CONTRACTING-OUT WILL BE INCREASINGLY AFFECTED BY THE USE OF HYBRID FORMS OF GUARD FORCE MANAGEMENT, IN WHICH THE CLIENT PLAYS A MORE ACTIVE ROLE IN HANDS-ON MANAGEMENT AND CONTROL.

Despite the inherent liability problems, hybrid forms of guard forces, in which proprietary supervisors exercise direct control over contract guards, will be seen much more frequently in the year 2000 than today. Particularly in cases involving the conversion of the in-house security forces to contract for cost reasons, such hybrid forces will prove attractive to an increasing number of security directors, principally because such arrangements are perceived to be much less of an "abdication" of control than an abrupt switch to an entirely contracted force. Contract security providers typically will not welcome this trend, both because of the muddled liability issues as well as the employment and labor relations problems that such forces sometimes create.

IN THE MOVE TO AN INFORMATION SOCIETY, THE TYPES OF MEDIA TO BE PROTECTED WILL REQUIRE FUNDAMENTAL CHANGES IN THE APPROACH, TRAINING AND METHODOLOGY OF THE PROTECTORS.

Protection of a smokestack industry plant requires materially different skills on the part of the security guard than does protection of a "think tank," computer center or research facility. Not that the protection principles differ so greatly, but the attitudes of those protected and the expectations that managers of such facilities have towards security officers and security forces dictate a somewhat different approach. Sensitivity to the subtle psychological issues will be but one of the requirements of the effective guard force of the 21st century. How well security providers react to these changes will dictate how well the guard of the 21st century is accepted as part of the increasingly knowledge-oriented future society.

ADVANCES IN ARTIFICIAL INTELLIGENCE WILL FURTHER ERODE THE GROWTH POTENTIAL OF THE GUARDING PROFESSION.

Guards traditionally have been employed to make discriminating judgments after analyzing situations and facts. The ability of computers to use increasingly sophisticated programs, which can analyze a wide variety of situations and initiate one or more courses of action for this analysis will increasingly take away from the utilization of guards. Indeed, in many cases, artificial intelligence can be expected to reliably and consistently make decisions in many situations (such as when to call the fire department, whether or not to sound certain alarms, under what circumstances to admit personnel to restricted areas, etc.) in which guard decisions in the past have been inconsistent or largely subjective. Notwithstanding that, it is unlikely that artificial intelligence will completely supplant some of the kinds of subjective judgments or intuitive decisions which are at times a necessary component of effective protection.

WOMEN WILL MAKE UP AN INCREASINGLY LARGER PROPORTION OF GUARD FORCES.

Before 1970, women were rarely seen as members of security forces. However, by 1982, according to the Bureau of Labor Statistics, some 82,000 women were employed in guard positions, an increase of 337% from 1972. Projecting increase in the proportion of women in security forces by the year 2000. A major impetus to the past increase in numbers of women has resulted from a lowering of barriers erected by these perceptions, resulting in a higher proportion of females in guarding positions by the turn of the century.

THE ADVANCE OF THE BABY BOOM GENERATION INTO THE EARLY RETIREMENT YEARS OFFERS THE CONTRACT SECURITY INDUSTRY A LARGE RESERVOIR OF

TALENT.

The average age of guards has been steadily declining since 1960. But much of the reason for that decline may well be reflected in what was happening to the general population during the period. Now, the population is aging in the United States, and it is not unreasonable to assume that the population of guard forces will mirror that trend.

FEW OF TODAY'S GUARDS WILL BE TOMORROW'S SECURITY DIRECTORS.

Although guards will be better trained and better educated than they are today, except in some select proprietary security organizations, few people who will rise to the top of security organizations will have begun their careers as a guard. Although there will be exceptions, the guard will remain an enlisted man in the security army, and despite the few who advance to become generals of their organizations, the vast majority will continue to occupy the lower rungs of the security ladder. Just as guards will require better training and more sophisticated skills to perform their jobs in the next century, so will security managers and guard company executives, and often the skills required by the latter groups will evolve and expand in ways different from those of the basic guard.

TOMORROW'S GUARD WILL BE OLDER AND BETTER EDUCATED THAN TODAY'S, BUT STILL POORLY PAID IN RELATION TO OTHER OCCUPATIONS.

The pressure of cheaper technologies will continue to exert a downward pressure on guard force wage rates. Security industry executives will come to realize that the major competition comes not from other firms, but from technologies that threaten to replace guards entirely. Wage boosts in proprietary organizations will be tempered both by technological advances as well as contract guard competition.

GUARDING WILL BE LESS RECESSION-RESISTANT THAN IN THE PAST DUE TO TECHNOLOGY'S ABILITY TO DO MORE THINGS WHICH WERE ONCE SOLELY THE PROVINCE OF HUMAN BEINGS.

For the first time, the deep recession in the early 1980s

awakened many contract guard providers to the fact that security was not immune from the business cycle. Until that point, there had been a general belief that even where there were production cutbacks, reduced work weeks and similar kinds of responses to a recession, security manpower would still be needed at substantially the same levels. However, the depth of the recession shattered that illusion. The security budget, in fact, became one of the first to be sliced and the area in which cutbacks could achieve the most significant results was in the reduction of manpower levels. Where protection was still required, the turn was accept greater risk by not protecting against certain hazards or, more likely, to rely upon electronics, a trend that can be expected to continue and accelerate in the event of recessions in the next century.

FEWER ACTS OF NONFEASANCE BY GUARDS WILL OCCUR, SINCE CONTROL SYSTEMS WILL BE MORE LIKELY TO DETECT THEM. SINCE NONFEASANCE WILL BE MORE LIKELY TO BE DETECTED, MARGINALLY PER-FORMING GUARDS, IMMUNE FROM DETECTION IN THE PAST, WILL BE MORE QUICKLY IDENTIFIED AND EITHER DISMISSED OR FAIL TO APPLY FOR GUARD POSITIONS IN THE FIRST PLACE. IN EITHER CASE, THE EFFECT ON GUARD TURNOVER AND RECRUITMENT WILL BE SIGNIF-ICANT.

It is reported that the watchman at Fords Theatre in Washington was carrying a watchclock similar to the one carried by most guards today when President Lincoln was shot in 1865. For more than 100 years, the means largely used to monitor whether guards patrolled properly has not changed. However, today new products are being seen in the marketplace which are revolutionizing guard tour reporting. Once guard tours are recorded electronically through hand-held devices and the information stored, the ability to sort that information in a meaningful way and provide exception reporting is clearly within reach. Dedicated hard-wired systems as well as hand-held systems used in a variety of different technologies, including bar code readers and magnetic sen-sors, coupled with computer analysis, have already shown the feasibility of tightly controlling guard performance. The expansion of such systems and the increasing sophistication of them suggests that the guard who fails to make rounds or who sleeps on posts by the year 2000 will have become a relic of the past. At the same time, such control and knowledge on the part of security managers will impel the most forward thinking managers to reevaluating the guard's job so as to make nonfeasance less likely.

THE CONCENTRATION OF CONTRACT GUARDING IN SEVERAL MEGA-GUARD FIRMS WILL CONTINUE, PLACING GREATEST PRESSURE NOT ON THE LOCAL FIRM, BUT ON THE MID-SIZE REGIONAL COMPANY.

The increase in expansion by acquisition of large national contract security firms will continue, particularly as the management of these companies recognize that it is often easier to buy guard hours sold by someone else rather than to sell them themselves.

The provision of contract guard services will remain a curiously personal business, with client retention often dependent much more upon the relationship between the local manager (or guard service company principal) and the client's local representative. Local companies with hands-on management, provided that they are otherwise competent, have historically had material advantages over either national or regional firms in the area of developing and maintaining client relationships. Larger companies, through greater financial resources, despite the added cost of layers of overhead, will still depend to a large extent on the effectiveness of their branch managers both to obtain new clients and retain them.

A wave of acquisitions has continued through the 1980s as a number of large guard firms, many of them having been acquired themselves by non-security conglomerates, continue their quest for larger sales and profit dollars. Typically, these firms are less interested in the small local firm than in the larger regional company, which can make their acquisition dollar go further. The regional firm additionally comes under the pressure of having expanded to the point were its local advantages often are as constraining as those of the national company on the one hand, but without the strong financial resources of the larger company on the other.

THE MARKET FOR PREMIUM GUARD SERVICES WILL HAVE GROWN, AS SOPHISTICATED AND COMPLEX CONTROL SYSTEMS DEMAND BETTER TALENT TO OPERATE. SHORTSIGHTED AND BUDGET-CONSCIOUS SECURITY DIRECTORS AND CORNER-CUTTING CONTRACT SECURITY PROVIDERS WILL UNWITTINGLY CONSPIRE TO IMPEDE WIDESPREAD DELIVERY OF SUCH PREMIUM SERVICES.

There is no sign that the age-old argument between security director and contract security provider relating to cost vs. value received will abate by the year 2000 or beyond. Although more and more sophisticated customers will come to recognize that better security manpower carries with it a cost, the limited ability of security directors to provide convincing arguments on this score to upper level management will continue to impede the purchase and delivery of higher quality services. On the other hand, contract security providers will continue to argue that they provide high quality service at lower cost, and in a competitive environment, often in the absence of clearly defined specifications, will deliver a product that does not meet often unrealistic expectations.

When the sole function of a guard was to patrol a deserted warehouse and punch a watch clock, the failings of marginal service were less noticeable. But as guards are called upon to use increasingly complex and sophisticated electronic and computer aids, inadequate selection training and supervision will become much more evident to clients.

SELECTION OF HONEST, RELIABLE GUARDS WILL BECOME INCREASINGLY DIFFICULT, DUE TO THE TREND, WHICH SHOWS NO SIGN OF ABATING, TOWARD PROTECTION OF APPLICANT PRIVACY. ALMOST EXCLUSIVE RELIANCE UPON AFTER-THE-FACT CRIMINAL HISTORY CHECKS WILL RESULT IN SEVERAL MAJOR GUARD DEFALCATIONS. THERE IS A SUBSTANTIAL LIKELIHOOD THAT AN INADEQUATELY SCREENED GUARD WILL BECOME A PRINCIPAL IN A TERRORIST INCIDENT WHICH COULD HAVE BEEN PREVENTED WITH ADEQUATE SCREENING.

Providers of guard services will find it increasingly difficult to hire honest, reliable guards, as many of the tools most useful to screening out the problem guard are taken away. By the year 2000, polygraph testing and psychological screening, as well as drug testing, will likely be prohibited. Restrictions on the use of credit bureau data will likewise become greater, as much through court decisions as from new legislation. Information from previous employers will be even less freely given than today as a result of increasing weariness on the part of employers who fear legal liability for information released. The sole means left for screening will likely be the criminal history check, which will prove an inadequate substitute for the more thorough, but by then proscribed, means of screening. Guard service providers as well as proprietary security forces will increasingly find themselves in the uncomfortable position of defending against actions based upon inadequate screening of guards while at the same time finding themselves even more unable than today to respond.

Just as history has often been made by the acts of a small number of people, so the act of a single guard may radically alter this projection. In 1960, for example, who would have thought that Americans would not only tolerate, but welcome, the intrusive universal searches now attendant to airline travel? A few dozen hijackers caused all that to happen. In much the same way, the acts of a few guards, out of hundreds of thousands of guards, could bring about radical changes in the security industry itself.

ABSENT A MAJOR INCIDENT (SUCH AS A TERRORIST INCIDENT) INVOLVING A GUARD, THE TREND TOWARD PRIVATIZATION WILL CONTINUE. HOWEVER THE TREND IS A FRAGILE ONE, WHICH CAN BE ALTERED BY A SINGLE MAJOR INCIDENT.

Numerous functions performed today by government may be converted by the year 2000 to performance by private industry, including the number of guard related activities. This trend, principally a result of economics, includes such tasks as conventional fixed post security duties, traffic control, enforcement of environmental regulations, court room protection, accident investigation and prisoner guarding. Privatization will not come easily and the degree of conversion from public to private services can be materially slowed by even a single serious incident that achieves widespread publicity with its attendant backlash.

These are but a few of the observable trends and projections that may affect the guard by the year 2000 and beyond. As our society changes and we move from the age of the industrial revolution into the age of information and knowledge, so, too, the protectors must evolve with it. The extent to which they and their leaders are able to adapt to and blend with the new technology and the changing attitudes of society will largely shape the continued important role which they will play.